NOT NORMAL
BEHAVIOUR

A catalogue record of this book is available from the British Library

First Edition: February 2005

ISBN: 1-84375-136-4

To order additional copies of this book please visit:
http://www.upso.co.uk/stuartstaples

Published by: UPSO Ltd
5 Stirling Road, Castleham Business Park,
St Leonards-on-Sea, East Sussex TN38 9NW United Kingdom
Tel: 01424 853349 Fax: 0870 191 3991
Email: info@upso.co.uk Web: http://www.upso.co.uk

NOT NORMAL BEHAVIOUR

FROM NOVICE TO ULTRA-DISTANCE TRIATHLETE

STUART STAPLES

UPSO

For Linds and Ben

Acknowledgments

There are a handful of people I truly count as friends who have helped me write this book. In particular I would like to mention Simon Howes, James Waller, Nicola Mulhaire and James and Anna Harrison for their advice and encouragement. Special thanks go to Jeannine Golding and Pip Pearson for their absolute diligence and attention to detail.

The importance of enjoying and getting the most from life was ingrained at an early age and for that I thank two people; my one true hero, my dad Ian, and his telepathic soul-mate, my mum Maggie.

With everything in perspective Ironman enriches my life. But in truth, it would be nothing without my best friend and wife, Linds.

Why *Not Normal Behaviour?*

Why the title *Not Normal Behaviour?* The inspiration for it came to me halfway through writing when I realised that perhaps I was behaving a little abnormally, not quite living my life in the conventional way. It was a dark, cold, wintry evening and we were at the in-laws, getting ready for Christmas. For that particular evening of the year, I wasn't where convention would have me. Whilst most people would be doing the last minute things you do on Christmas Eve, I was dressed up in full winter running gear, on a footpath alongside the Wetherby Bypass, doing 90 second speed intervals. There I was, alone, on a partially lit footpath, battling with a steady side-wind, the odd car flying by, happy and absorbed, feeling really alive. I smiled. Behaving abnormally was a rich way to live.

This is the story of my less than conventional lifestyle from June 2000 to July 2001 and the highs and the lows of becoming an ultra-distance triathlete.

PART 1

The Novice

Chapter 1

Iron Man

Every adventure has a beginning and mine burst forth from the addled shell of the 'Ground Force' dream. One of my best mates, Neil, and I had just finished building a three brick high seating area with a neat gravel bed in my back garden. He disputes how much time I spent on the actual building per-say. I, on the other hand, am absolutely adamant he would never have laid all those bricks single-handedly if it wasn't for my mortar mixing and tea making skills. The ungrateful swine.

Well anyway, contractor disputes aside, upon completion there I sat, smug and content, with a warm DIY self-improvement glow. A blue sky stretched above me and I was tanning on a wooden garden chair, a couple of cushions easing the hardness of the wood. I'd pulled my shorts low so I wouldn't get an obvious tan line. With suncream on, a book, a cold drink and my shades, this was suburbia.

You could have almost panned upwards, away from the garden and looked down on the house, the neat moss ravaged lawn and the newly constructed, brick-lined seating area. Up higher still to see a neat housing estate in Milton Keynes, with lots of roundabouts, a grid system and virtually no traffic jams. Neat, and there I was sweating. It was very hot, early June 2000. I had never been further from adventure. And with that thought I actually felt a little cold, a little small and a little insignificant. Where had this come from? How could I not be happy sitting there surrounded by my greatest legacy, the world's biggest gravel filled cat litter?

I was reading Pete Goss's 'Close to the Wind'. This book was part of a long series of armchair adventures about Everest, the Antarctic, the Arctic, jungles, hostile places and life endangering challenges. Goss's account of his trip was inspiring. He was constantly facing failure, defeat, rejection, poverty and misery and most of this hardship was before he even set sail. The account on the high seas was even more inspiring. As I sat there, sweating in my neat little garden, it struck me that my level of challenge wasn't enough. I wanted to get out of my garden chair and face a little more hardship than whether I had enough suncream on my chest and toes. My mind was set. I had never been more certain of anything. It was time to up the ante from rather safe and un-ambitious landscape gardening projects.

To describe my multi-sport CV as anything more than patchy would be flattering it. Basically, in its very simplest terms, despite my swagger, I had been dabbling with triathlon for about six months. Even dabbling seems an over-generous description. I had finished the Spelthorne Sprint triathlon (400 metre swim, 12 mile bike ride and 3 mile run) which amounted to about an hour and 10 minutes of exercise. As far as challenges went, it had been a bit longer than a game of squash. Not exactly radical. I was deluding myself. I had a race T-shirt and I thought I was the dogs' bollocks. Compared to Goss, I was a complete sissy. Suddenly I felt I was missing out on a whole world of adventure.

It was beyond me why, but it struck me that I had to do something totally insane. I had to set out to do something I felt would be impossible. But what? Then it hit me like a bolt. Ironman. I knew very little about Ironman. I had a vague idea of the distance. It was a long way, just short of a two and a half mile swim, 112 miles on the bike and finally a marathon. Wow. Each leg on its own seemed enormous. I thought about it. 2.4 miles, 112 miles, 26.2 miles. That's a long way from normal. I had images of epic battles of endurance between scantily clad men and women, all bronzed and muscled. I knew I wanted to pull myself out of my neat housing estate and join these lycra sporting ranks.

When Neil had asked a few months before where I was going with triathlon (yeah, with one sprint event under my belt, I had deluded myself I was going somewhere with it), I replied that I thought I'd get into Olympic distance races, (1 mile swim, 25 mile bike ride and 6 mile run) but I thought doing an Ironman would be totally nuts, only for fools and the stupid. When I said this to him I had meant it. With my minimal experience and triathlon credentials, doing an Ironman would be crazy. And that simply was the appeal. A task too massive to contemplate. It was so far from where I was then, so out of my comfort zone, such a big challenge, the simplicity made the decision easy. I would do an Ironman. I felt a tingle, a surge of excitement. I guess it was a purpose. Thanks Pete. I finished his book and miraculously didn't burn my toes.

Now the decision to do one was easy, but where would I start? How would I go about entering a race? Choose an event, I thought. But how? The whole thing seemed to be shrouded in mystery. It was a world I knew nothing about. I didn't even know anyone who had done one. But with the decision made I had to find out more so I turned to the Internet. Into the search engine I entered, 'Ironman'. I was sent to a site called 'ironmanlive.com'. I read on, hungry to know more. This was a good site detailing all I needed to know. Well, almost. It listed the events. There was something about a World Championship in Hawaii, this being the Mecca of Ironman, and you having to qualify (qualify!) through one of a number of other worldwide Ironman events. Qualifying events? Would I need to qualify to get into these? Oh my god, this wasn't going to be as straightforward as I'd thought. It all sounded very hardcore. But I had a passion in my belly. I felt compelled and I knew I had to complete one. That was that. I would have to put my name down, pay my money and see myself on a list. That would seal my resolve. Then there would be nowhere to run. The seed was sown in my mind as I stared at the website. I read on. I had set myself the challenge of finishing an Ironman.

The next question was when? Now I was foolhardy, but not completely dumb. I knew I would have to build up to it by training hard. I would have to look at the next 12 to 14 months.

As I said, I had a vague idea of what to expect but however I looked at the distances, they sounded a long way. Actually each leg back to back sounded impossible. How far could I swim? I could swim a mile doing front crawl. Well 60 lengths of a 25 metre pool, therefore was it really a mile with all the pushing off? Had I really swum a mile continuously? No. Did I enjoy swimming? No, it seemed to take forever. I wasn't improving and swimming was by far my worst event. To go from 1 mile to 2.4 miles and then add a bike ride which was further than I had ever ridden before, and follow this with a marathon, seemed nuts.

What was the furthest I had ever cycled? I'd cycled 106 miles; in fact I had cycled that far on two separate occasions. But had I felt like running after those rides? No way. All I'd wanted to do was sit in a chair, drink cool milk and eat chocolate. Could I have done a marathon afterwards? I could barely walk up the stairs.

Had I ever run a marathon? Yes, I ran the London Marathon in 1999 in a very respectable 3 hours 34 minutes. And that hurt. I can remember Tower Bridge coming around very quickly and feeling good up until the 14 mile mark, then my legs getting heavier. I remember slowing until about 19 miles, then 19 to 25 miles taking forever. I remember it mostly for the fact that it was a long way.

I'll be honest, I wasn't a total fat lardy bastard. From the age of about thirteen I had been passionate about sport. My inspiration came from watching a rather naff film, about two brothers taking part in a cycle race, called *The Hell of the West*, which captured all the thrills of road racing. That very same summer I saw the Tour de France for the first time. Cycling suddenly seemed like a fantastic sport. Whilst most of my friends had Spurs or Liverpool football shirts, I had a replica cycling jersey. I borrowed my Dad's racer and started imagining I was either King of the Mountains, out alone in a suicidal breakaway or beating the Pelaton (the main pack) in a ferocious sprint. Cycling has been a passion ever since. But to say I was any good would be misleading. I was distinctly average, I wasn't quick, my training was erratic and I had no natural talent. But I *was* fit.

The fitness I gained in my early teens put me in good stead. I loved playing rugby and the strength I picked up seemed to give me an advantage over my peers. When I got into a little trouble at school, aged fourteen, Dad packed me off to Tae Kwon Do in an attempt to persuade the headmaster to give me a second chance. It worked and it gave me a sport I loved for the next five years and further reason to stay fit and strong. During my teens I was either cycling, running, playing rugby, practising Tae Kwon Do or studying for school. At seventeen I stopped playing rugby after a neck and back injury had me whisked from the pitch. I had quite a fright on the X-ray table as they checked for permanent spinal damage. With a vertebrae dislodged, my rugby days were over but I came back determined to get fit so upped my cycling and running.

Going to university forced me to drop Tae Kwon Do but found me turning religiously to circuit training, keep fit, aerobics and step classes. I got so addicted I ended up becoming qualified to teach classes, although I always maintained I was a fitness instructor rather than an aerobics teacher. They were fantastic years and I found myself in my early twenties pretty much addicted to keeping fit and exercise.

Whilst at university I also met Linds, my best friend and wife, probably the world's most patient and tolerant person, especially when it comes to my obsessions. After graduating, we found ourselves in Milton Keynes. Linds had a proper job and I started out temping and wondering why I had studied so hard at university. But it was here in Milton Keynes, one of the furthest points from the sea, I found my next obsession, windsurfing. I quickly became a junkie, constantly watching weather forecasts, keeping an eye on trees, flags, any tell-tale signs that we were in for a blow. Every spare penny I had went into buying gear. It was the perfect sport to compliment my cycling as I didn't enjoy riding in the wind. Miraculously Linds stuck with me, sitting in cars on windswept beaches on the most awful days of the year. We went out when there was snow on the ground. If it was windy I would sail.

Some people accused me of having an addictive personality. Maybe. I felt it was more a tendency to really get into things I enjoyed. My entry into the London Marathon had been a last minute thing. A friend, 'Psycho' Dave, called me five weeks before the start to say his brother had dropped out and would I take his charity spot. Without hesitation I accepted. That rather rash decision would prove to be one of the most influential of my life. Despite the pain, or perhaps because of it, I loved it and wanted to do more endurance events. Almost the day after the marathon I went back to running and my knees flared up. So while I recuperated I jumped into the pool to keep my fitness up. After a few sessions the idea of competing in a sprint triathlon was born. Without really realising it, my whole life had been on a crash course destined to arrive at that moment in my garden. I had always pushed myself but not really understood why. In June 2000 I was to start a new adventure but I still didn't understand why.

So I was fitness fanatic, a gym bore, some would probably say I exercised to excess. The next 12 months would prove otherwise. I would learn that there are loads of people who follow the same pattern, many of whom do far more than me and are also much better at it. Initially they are hard to spot as they keep themselves to themselves, but if you look you'll find them, especially in the fast lane of the swimming pool. I didn't venture there often. It damaged my confidence too much to be lapped by a swimmer every eight to ten lengths. Sometimes I was lapped every four lengths, which was totally soul-destroying. There was nothing worse than a graceful swimmer effortlessly passing me whilst I was dying and flaying with exhaustion. When this occurred, as it frequently did, the torpedo that had just flown by would typically add insult to injury by disabling their legs with a float and swim using only their arms. My only point of reference to the fact that I wasn't laying face down stationary in the pool, was that the bottom would be passing slowly below me. As I've said, I wasn't keen on swimming, and I certainly wasn't strong at it.

I knew if I was to be successful I needed to get a plan together. I needed to find out how much training would be required to enable me to go the distance. When I thought about it, it was overwhelming. But I still had the tingle inside. I knew I had found something which would challenge and stretch me. Something from which I would draw huge satisfaction. Not by winning. But by standing on the start line and hopefully crossing the finish. Thanks Pete. I knew I was starting out on an adventure. The next 12 months would tell me whether I was made of 'the right stuff'. I didn't know whether I would succeed or what I'd learn, but I was excited. I had a challenge, my own adventure. No more 'armchair athlete'. No more Scott of the Antarctic, Mallory or Shackleton. I would be turning my own pages in this adventure. I went to tell Linds about my revelation. She listened patiently, her eyes rolled in a resigned fashion as if to say, 'Here we go again'.

Chapter 2

The Paper Triathlete

The concept of Ironman was born back in 1977 in Hawaii. The original race happened as a result of an argument between some US Navy sailors about who was the fittest; a swimmer, a cyclist or a runner. John Collins, the founder of the race, determined that only through the combination of the island's three toughest endurance events; the Waikiki Rough Water Swim, the Around Oahu Bike Race and the Honolulu Marathon, could they really conclude who was fittest. With little preparation, on February 12th 1978, 12 competitors set out. With no marshals and no outside support nine competitors finished and they were all declared iron men. The race remained low key until 1980 when a television crew from ABC caught the startling images of Julie Moss, the lead female, collapse within sight of the finishing line. As she crawled towards glory her main rival passed her to take the prize. The legend, the drama, the mystique of Ironman was beamed across the world. Some twenty years on, triathlon has gone from strength to strength.

There are four main triathlon distances:

Sprint – 400 to 750 metre swim, 12 mile bike ride and 3 mile run
Olympic – 1 mile swim, 25 mile bike ride and 6 mile run
Half-Ironman – 1.2 mile swim, 56 mile bike ride and 13.1 mile run
Ironman, the daddy of them all – 2.4 mile swim, 112 mile bike ride and 26.2 mile run

I had done a Sprint and was still very much a novice, a long way from the legends of Hawaii. It was early June, about a week after my sunbathing revelation and I was like a man possessed. In truth, life had continued as ever but with a new and exciting dream in my head. Ironman. Seven days into my career as an ultra athlete and I was very pleased with my progress. Well, that's if you consider progress to be telling a few friends and colleagues that I planned to do an Ironman. Outwardly nothing much had changed. I had gone to work as usual. Work was work. I was hardly Wall Street's Gordon Geko; braces, striped shirt and gelled back hair. In terms of my career there was no real master plan. I had come to do what I was doing more by chance than by design. I was a salesman. A somewhat inexperienced salesman, but I was a salesman nonetheless. It was an easy enough job. I lived five miles from the office, therefore had no stressful commuting. I was earning money and felt I was making my way in life. In reality, I was treading water.

Before you get the violin out, I had nothing to complain about really, but there was something missing. Here I was in my late twenties and I just felt like a matchstick man; I was driving to work, parking my car, filing into the office, doing my job and then filing out and driving home. Was this it? Well, it was this and minor construction projects at the weekend, where I would play second fiddle and tea boy. I had woken up and for the last week I had lived with real purpose. At least in spirit. There was still a long way to go.

It was time to ratify my status as a triathlete. As I wasn't a member of a club and didn't know any other triathletes, I decided I needed some help. My first objective was to join an association so I joined the British Triathlon Association (BTA). Now I have got to say all of a sudden this was getting pretty cool. Admittedly I didn't need to prove anything, but there was still a bit of a thrill in becoming a member. Why? Let's put it this way, there is a certain amount of kudos in having an association certify me as a triathlete. Yeah, I was shallow but hey, it's a fact that;

Triathletes are hard men and women. They are endurance athletes. They shave their bodies and train all hours of the day. They have six pack stomachs, lean legs and arms. And the coolest thing ever is, when they race, they have their race number written on their body.

For £30 and the price of a phone call, I had joined this exclusive club. Easy really. I hadn't been asked to prove all the above prerequisites and somehow with 1 hour and 10 minutes of racing behind me, I was an official triathlete. Well, at least on paper. I couldn't wait for the card in my wallet. I'd always been averse to stickers in cars, but maybe I could make an exception.

Whilst I was buoyed by my progress, good old Neil brought me crashing back to earth. 'What about training?' A membership card and a sticker were hardly going to get me through a marathon. In fact they would do little to get my flaying graceless swimming technique to the start of the bike course and they would be next to useless slogging out 112 miles. But I didn't panic. I'd always been interested in keeping fit, going to the gym and staying trim, but I needed a little of Neil's laconic observation to realise I was now entering a whole new world.

So there I was in the BTA. They were friendly enough and tried to be helpful, but in truth they seemed to do little more than issue cards and car stickers. They didn't know much about Ironman and advised me to look online. Ah - back to the Internet. I sat there in my lunch hour (honest) and plugged in 'Ironman' again and again, searching for new and different sites. Slowly my knowledge grew, and with it my concerns. The task was enormous. I learned with incredulity that you are given 17 hours to complete the event. 17 hours of continuous exercise. I could probably count the number of times I have stayed awake that long on both hands. But still it was 17 hours. This broke down into 2.5 hours to complete the swim, 10.5 hours to complete the combined swim and the bike ride and finally 17 hours to complete the whole event. I did a few calculations. It didn't take a genius to work out that 17 hours is a long time, it's 71% of a day. Again I think the genius would conclude that's a long time to subject your body to continuous exertion. But, and I thought 'but' with slight trepidation, if I could keep my body going for that time, I was bound to cover the distance. Oh yes, I was foolhardy even at this stage. The unknown question was, could I keep my body ticking over the distance at the pace required? Ticking over? Idiot, moving at a fair speed.

But hope springs eternal, especially in the world of the foolhardy. I just needed to enter a race. I needed to find a race towards the back end of summer 2001. I figured I would be able to get sufficient racing experience in for the rest of 2000 and build my fitness. I knew training outdoors during the winter months in the UK was no fun, but all I needed to do was wrap up warm and just get out there. Then in the following spring, I would launch the main offensive through to my longest day in late summer 2001. So simple.

Now, the next question was which Ironman event? I was looking for the 'easiest', ideally over a flat course for the bike section and free from wind. I know, a contradiction really. I was looking for a gruelling event, but trying to reduce the gruel as much as possible. Foolhardy I may have been, but I wasn't completely gung ho. I wanted to be sensible (I guess everything is relative).

So with these preferences in mind, I sat down and read the course profiles and descriptions of all the major Ironman events. Gradually I was narrowing my options. There were 22 Ironman events around the world in some exotic locations. I read on, and then I nearly fell of my chair;

'The level of training that athletes should be looking at whilst training for an Ironman is; 7 miles swimming per week, 240 miles cycling and 45 miles running.'

I felt a little numb. Hello. Do these people have jobs? Do they sleep? How can you train that much a week? I didn't have an answer.

And a far more pressing concern than an Ironman 14 months away was the small matter of the Windsor Olympic Distance Triathlon, in just over a week's time, that I had been spending the spring and early summer working towards.

I logged off. Being a triathlete on paper was one thing. Little help my membership card and car sticker would give me in the fast current of the Thames.

Chapter 3

Wear A Swim Hat

So there I was, a week before Windsor, standing on the bank of a lake about to take the plunge. I was seven days away from a 1 mile swim, a 25 mile bike ride and a 6 mile run. The bike and the run held little fear for me, but the prospect of swimming a mile in the murky Thames against the current? Yep, I was dreading it.

I had never done an open water swim before, especially in a river. I knew I could cover the distance, but could I swim it in a wetsuit? In a wetsuit against the current in one of the country's dirtiest rivers? To say I was feeling apprehensive would be an understatement. What would happen if I got stuck in the same place? I could just imagine it, churning the strokes frantically, kicking like a donkey and barely moving forward, or even worse moving backwards. What was more, there would be a herd of far more experienced triathletes in a mass start doing their utmost to leave me behind. How would I cope in a tightly confined group start? The fear was magnified yet further by the fact that the event would be televised and, worse still, I had foolishly invited my proud Grandma along to unwittingly witness my humiliation.

So with my thick winter windsurfing wetsuit, goggles and trunks in hand, I jumped into the car and headed down to the local windsurfing lake at Brogborough to give open water swimming a go.

Full of confidence I pulled on my wetsuit and swaggered out of the car park with all the bravado I felt a triathlete should possess. I skirted around the side of the lake, wetsuit zipped tight, goggles in hand and neoprene boots on to avoid any pre-race injuries. I found a suitable place to launch my open water swimming career, beyond the main windsurfing 'drag' strip, where I would be safe. There, on the grassy bank, I removed my boots and nervously, for fear of treading on something sharp, entered the water. Everything seemed fine. I pulled on my mirrored Speedo goggles and I was ready to fly.

I launched myself into the murk. Whoa, it was cold on the head. Panic. My head popped up. It wasn't like the tranquillity of the pool. Oh no. Where were the lanes? Where was the bottom? Where was the clear blue water? Open water swimming was going to be a very, very different kettle of fish. The bravado of, hey I am a triathlete, quickly evaporated.

Standing not five feet from the bank and my neatly ordered boots, I cursed myself for my lack of nerve. Come on, swim, I thought, you'll quickly warm up. With gritted teeth I ducked my head back in and started to front crawl. I set myself a point and struck out for it. Needless to say I didn't get there. My head went up, my feet went down, I kicked, treading water, gulping air. Maybe I got about a third of the way; maybe if I am honest it was a quarter. Whatever it was, I was blown away.

No doubt about it, open water swimming was intimidating. The wind chop was in my face, in my mouth, up my nose, suffocating my breathing, pushing against my strokes. I could feel the cold of the water on my feet and hands, the waves breaking over my head. The murkiness of the water meant I was hardly able to see my hands and had no idea where the bottom was. Could I put my feet down? Would I want to? The thick winter wetsuit was limiting my movements and making my arms and legs powerless. It was the isolation, the loneliness, the vastness of the apparent nothingness below me. I definitely didn't enjoy it one bit and I couldn't get over the feeling of panic. I turned and headed for the shore, deflated. What I thought would be a walk in the park was proving altogether different. My dread of the Thames magnified. I realised I faced utter humiliation before my Grandma. Suddenly it all felt very difficult. I felt very small.

I sat on the bank and caught my breath, the warmth of the sun beating down on my face. Flies landed on my suit. Was it really that bad? Maybe the first one is always the worst. I looked down the lake. Was I really ready to commit to this sport? I decided to have another go at the swim and this time to set a less ambitious target.

I launched and swam through the weed growing close to the shore. Come on, you are getting into this, I encouraged myself. Arms turn, legs kick, head rotates and breathe. Better? No. A wave broke in my open mouth. Agghh, head up, treading water, rhythm broken, cough, choke, deep breath. Come on, get your head down, you can do it. Don't let this stop your Ironman. Hey forget the Ironman, you've got the Thames in a week.

I had to make this work. I stopped treading water and kicked forward again into the front crawl position. This time I kept my head up a little higher to help me breathe. My legs sank but I moved forward. I was swimming, but not enjoying it. I reached my point and turned. My arms were tired, my legs felt useless. In the shallows, I wobbled to my boots and sat down, labouring for breath. Stillness again, sheltered from the wind by the bank. A mile in the Thames in a week's time. I knew I needed to go out again. So I did, but not immediately. When I returned to my boots for the third and final time I felt exactly the same. Overwhelmed, intimidated and not ready.

Rather than a swagger back to the car park jubilant in my success, it was more of a dejected shuffle. The victory I had anticipated over open water swimming had ended in an absolute routing. Lake 3 – Me 0. I knew I couldn't settle for this. My resolve hardened. I had to overcome this. Could it really be that hard? Could it really be that different from pool swimming? Yes, yes, yes. I was glad I had gone down. Far better to find out there than wait until I was washed out to sea from Windsor.

I drove home, shell-shocked. The Ironman seemed a long way away. The swim had knocked me back, I just hadn't expected it. I thought about it. Why had I panicked? I tried to analyse it. Suddenly it came to me. I should have worn a swim hat. I went immediately to the local sports shop and bought a hat. I returned to the lake the following evening. I pulled on my new hat and swam about half a mile. I wouldn't call it a victory, but maybe it was a draw.

Why did a hat make a difference? I think it closed out the nasty, vast, cold world that is the 'shark/monster attack from below', the deep emptiness of the water. The waves are less intense, the noise is quieter and the cold isn't as sharp on the head. In a swim hat I was protected. It felt like I was in my own world. Yes, the water was still murky and I could barely see beyond the end of my arm. The weed still clung, the wetsuit drained my power and the waves pushed me back, but there was a calmness within the cocoon of my hat. A certain tranquillity.

Open water swimming was another world. There was still a long way to go, but I felt better about Windsor, safe in my hat.

Chapter 4

Everything But The Kitchen Sink

At last it was the morning before Windsor 2000. It was going to be a hot weekend. Despite my BTA membership card and all my talk, I was still well and truly a multi-sport novice and Windsor was my first real foray into the world of triathlon. I was very excited and had told nearly everyone I knew that I was competing. Over the Thursday and the Friday there had been a string of messages from friends and family wishing me good luck. How could I fail now?

All week the doubts had whirled through my head. Was I ready? I wasn't sure, but I thought so. I had been a little daunted by the instructions which arrived mid week. Reading them on the journey down, in our car loaded up to the gunnels, I concluded we had a complicated day ahead. It was such a big event, with about 900 people taking part, that you couldn't just roll up on the Sunday morning and set your bike up. 'All athletes' I read with pride 'must register and rack bikes the day before the race.'

The adventure was beginning. As we hurtled down the M1, I was sure I'd left nothing to chance. The previous evening I had packed my bag, checked my bike and made sure all my energy drinks were ready. Looking back, I may have packed in excess of my requirements. My kit bag contained: 3 pairs of cycling shorts, 2 pairs of swimming trunks, 3 running vests, 4 pairs of socks, 2 cycling shirts, my trainers, cycling shoes, helmet, 2 pairs of Oakley sunglasses, 3 towels (1 for standing on as I changed shoes, 1 for wiping the worst of the water off after the swim and finally 1 for drying myself after the race), goggles, swim hat and finally 2 sweatshirts for after the race if, I was cold.

I shudder with embarrassment now. In addition, as we were staying with my Grandma who lives near Windsor, I had my 'going out with Grandma the night before' togs and my 'getting to and from the race' clothes. I was leaving nothing to chance. It was a miracle the suspension on our little Renault Clio could take it.

Now, my attention to detail had catered for every eventuality, and one critical decision had been my T-shirt wardrobe for registration. Somewhat superficially, as I queued to register, I felt it necessary to flaunt my previous racing triumphs, scant though they were. So after limited deliberation (it was either the London Marathon or Spelthorne Sprint Triathlon) I settled for London, confident I would avoid any sartorial faux pas.

Anyway, I digress. The day was a scorcher. Brimming with nerves in an over-packed Clio, bike on the back, we pulled off the M4 into the outskirts of Windsor. Here was our first lesson; read all the registration details before getting to your destination. We pulled up on to the bank of the river where the transition area was, only to find that the registration point was about six miles away in Slough. We had made the rookie mistake of following the first car we saw with a 'British Triathlon Association' sticker in the back window and a driver wearing wrap around shades. We were turned back to Slough by a friendly policeman. The day was getting hotter. We were both hungry. I was nervous.

We parked outside the hotel in Slough. I took my registration details, ID and BTA card into the registration hall, where there also happened to be a triathlon exhibition (Expo). For the uninitiated, a triathlon exhibition is an area full of stands selling triathlon gear. This usually includes all the essential items such as skimpy lycra clothing, wetsuits, bikes, bits for the bike, carbon fibre wheels, and pretty much anything else you can imagine. With all the triathlon gear and tanned, fit, shaven folks wandering around, I felt like I'd stepped into the photos of my well-thumbed Triathlon magazines. I was like a kid in a sweet shop and also felt a bit of a fraud. I couldn't help feeling I was way out of my league and half expected a sympathetic official to kindly take me aside, a little embarrassed, and with a reassuring hand on my arm, say, 'Look we saw your efforts last week in the lake and, I don't know how best to say this, but for safety reasons we think it's best if you don't compete.' I kept my eyes down hoping not to be spotted.

Mindful of premature elimination and Linds' hunger, I wanted to be as quick as possible. I had my helmet inspected, no problems there. Then I checked the competitor lists and queued in the corresponding line for my number, 316. I was given a green wristband that would let me in and out of transition, a helmet and bike number and two pin-on-numbers to decorate my front and back. To time the event, we were all given a champion chip. These are timing devices which must be worn around your ankle so when you go over mats they can record your time. I was also given a plastic bag of goodies and my race T-shirt. Excellent, I would be safe for my next triathlon. Despite Linds sitting cooking in the car, on bike watch duty, I made a quick circuit of the Expo. Jubilant about my success at avoiding safety conscious officials, I raced out with two cans of coke to save my poor beloved before she went crispy. I was praying it would be warm for the following day.

What next? Put my bike in the appropriate rack in the transition area. We drove back into Windsor. Fortunately, due to my previous schoolboy error, we knew exactly where to go and parked up again by the river with relative ease. I had a quick look at the speed of the current. No doubt about it, it looked fast. I regretted not making more of an effort to get spotted by one of the safety conscious officials back in Slough. Was this wilful neglect, letting novices like me into this torrent? Maybe the PR machine could handle a few deaths. Better that than refund me my entry fee. With these dark thoughts I took my bike off the back of the car and passed through some trees into the transition area. This was impressive. The whole area was surrounded by high mesh fencing and manned by security. I had truly arrived in triathlon heaven. Here we were, in the centre of a transition area equivalent to the size of a football pitch, lined with bike racks with some awesome looking bikes. I felt like a little boy on his first day at school. Here were all these shiny carbon fibre bikes with aerobars and disc wheels. And there I was on a 10 year old Peugeot Optimum 14 speed racer. This lightly shaded purple steed had been the pride and joy of my late teens but had now become the lilac coloured slightly rusting shame of my blooming triathlon career. I had no aerobars, the gear shifters were down on the frame and the paintwork was scratched, bubbling and corroding in places due to years of turbo training (a static indoor trainer) and neglect. It would do the job but compared with the steeds all around, it looked like a penny-farthing.

We followed the crowds and ended up at the entrance to the racking area. I put my bike sticker on the handlebars and walked into the racking zone. All the racks were marked with numbers and I placed my bike in the appropriate spot. As you can imagine, it looked a bit forlorn.

Beside the racking area was another tented exhibition. My credit card could take a real hammering here. But food must prevail. I went back to see Linds and finally we had something to eat. I read the race pack while we ate. There was a race briefing at 4.30 and I had a sneaky feeling it would be a good idea to attend. After eating, we had a look around the Expo and then took a walk up the swim course. We walked three quarters of a mile up the river bank to the turn buoy. Even walking along the bank it seemed a long way. As we stood by the river's edge, the muddy water slid endlessly by and visions of me being swept downstream, completely powerless, filled me with dread. Still, I was glad I looked and prepared myself because the next day it seemed even longer and the current even stronger. It was here that I was well and truly beaten in the game of T-shirt poker. I'd thought my marathon T-shirt would impress my peers, but as I strutted up the swim course, my eyes landed on the coolest T-shirt ever. It simply said, 'Lanzarote Ironman – Finisher'. This guy, tanned, toned and with chiselled features, made my marathon T-shirt look like I'd worn a Michael Bolton T-shirt to an ACDC gig. Once again an Ironman felt a long way off.

With all the preparation it had been a frantic day and there was a huge risk of wearing myself out before I even got to the start line. So, happy in the sun, we just sat by the transition area and waited for the briefing. As the time got nearer our secluded, quiet area started to fill up with, I was relieved to see, a large number of equally nervous people. Maybe I wasn't the only new boy in school. There was an excited atmosphere, a tension building. It was a great feeling. While we sat there, Tim Don, Britain's number one hopeful at the time, walked through as well as other athletes I recognised from the pages of the monthly triathlon bible, 220 magazine. The briefing started. John Lunt, head of the Human Race organisation (an organisation which stages a number of triathlons and duathlons in the UK), took us through all the details. He explained how and when we could access transition in the morning for those final preparations and checks, how the swim starts would work, the swim course, the exit point from the water and the run through to transition. He described the bike course, any potential dangers and the rules of the road (basically follow the Highway Code and don't run red lights). He also warned us about drafting, in simple terms this is slip-streaming the bike in front of you, for which you would be penalised. He then described the run course, the finishing set up and finally took questions. I had resolved, after my second open water swim in Brogborough, that my full winter wetsuit was too restrictive to swim a mile in, so I was going to wear my shortie, a thinner summer wetsuit with short arms and legs. I knew it would be colder but I couldn't face the claustrophobic feeling of trying to swim a mile in a thick wetsuit. John said I would be fine. No excuses now.

After the briefing we decided to drive the bike course and then make our way to Grandma's. The course seemed a long way and fairly undulating in the car. However, the ride into Windsor was impressive and, importantly, downhill. I felt ready. We drove to Grandma's, showered, changed and went out for dinner. I was careful with what I ate and got to bed early. I would be lying if I said I slept well.

Chapter 5

Race Day

The alarm went off. It was 5.30am. I hadn't slept much. Jangling nerves. Why was I putting myself through this? I had a cup of tea and a couple of cereal bars, a quick shower and I was ready to go. Poor Linds and Grandma. If I couldn't see the point in getting up this early, what hope did they have?

Having said that, we were all very excited. This was my first proper triathlon. Grandma was teeming with pride. I think Linds was as well although, not being a morning person, she was playing it cool. At least that's what I took the groaning to mean. I had my pre-departure trip to the toilet and we jumped in the car and were on our way. Triathlons have unearthly starts. The most horrific start times were those of the ladies and the age groupers as their gun went off at 6.30am. My start was just before 8am. We arrived in Windsor just before 7am, parked on the outskirts of town and took a courtesy bus into the centre.

Fortunately, Linds is very unselfish and she looked after Grandma, as all I could think about was myself. Despite the early hour, Windsor was alive with energy and people. The transition area was buzzing with excitement. It was a big day for a lot of people. I went into transition and found my bike, slightly disappointed that no one had pinched it in the night. I set up my transition. Now, I had put a lot of thought into this. I laid out a towel on the floor. I would need my cycling stuff first so I put these bits at the front. Despite the broad choice of clothing and all the spares I had in my bag, I only put down my cycling shoes, one pair of socks, my vest with numbers attached, my helmet and sunglasses.

I would wear my cycling shorts under my wetsuit. Behind this I set up my running kit. I made sure my trainers were unlaced. I placed one bottle of isotonic drink on my bike. This would prove to be a mistake as it was a hot ride and I was left thirsty towards the end. I had one final look over the transition area and then went to the exit. From here I made sure that I knew where my bike was, counting up the racks and sections down on my row. I then made sure I knew where the exits were. I was ready.

I left the rest of my kit with Linds and Grandma and went for a gentle warm-up jog. I felt the urge to 'pay a visit' again. I ran down to the loo. They were all out of paper. Disaster. Oh well, needs must. I walked into the Ladies, apologising profusely, and grabbed a handful of paper. Relieved, and vowing to always take a roll of toilet paper with me to future events, I went back to my support crew. 15 minutes left until my start. The butterflies were dancing in my belly now.

We went to the riverside, I squeezed into my shortie, pulled my swim hat over my head and put some Vaseline on my neck. After a final stretch, I gave Linds and Grandma a kiss, pulled on my goggles and, like a condemned man, lowered myself into the Thames.

Christ, it was cold, and the current was strong. I pushed off from the concrete bank to try a few tentative strokes. My movement was a lot easier in the shortie. Good choice, or at least so I thought until I tried a proper tri-wetsuit 10 months later. The water was a dirty, thick brown colour and the current tugged me backwards. I swam back and forth to get used to the water and then clung onto a ring on the bank to stop from drifting (or should I say being swept) downstream. There was quite a crowd on the bank. I gave Linds and Grandma a little wave and shivered from the cold. Mmmmm, this was fun! I had to get in the zone. The countdown to the gun began, the water tugged at me and there I clung to my ring. The field seemed split into two groups as the clock ticked down; those who appeared to know what they were doing and who were swimming desperately to stay on the line to gain the greatest advantage, and then the rest of us, the 'also-rans', clinging for dear life onto rings and ropes, anything to conserve energy for what lay ahead. The water was cold, impenetrably dirty and flowing relentlessly away from where I wanted to go.

The gun sounded. There was a splash, a flurry of strokes and we were off. The course crossed the river to the other bank. I swam on, the current pulling at me, the dirty water obscuring my vision. My fears of the infamous mass start, kicking, punching and fighting with my fellow competitors evaporated as I quickly found myself swimming virtually alone. Most of the field had taken off and I was left to claw my way through the seemingly murky treacle of the Thames. I kicked and splashed on. Keep your mouth shut. Try and stay with someone's feet. If they pull away, try and stay with someone else's feet. The official had said stay close to the bank. Was I close enough? It appeared the answer to that question was no.

I kicked and pulled on. Keep your mouth shut. Every so often I would accidentally let a little water into my mouth. I choked, gagged and spat it out. The swim was taking forever. I passed under the first bridge and could then see the next one just behind the turn buoy. It was hard work. I took in another mouthful of water and started gagging again. Keep swimming. The right chamber of my goggles had gradually filled with water and with every turn of my head it ran back and forth across my open eye. It was claustrophobic, suffocating. It seemed as if the second bridge would never arrive. 'Just keep going', I told myself. Eventually, after what seemed like a lifetime, I got to the turn buoy. It had taken forever and then I realised why.

As I turned around the buoy and started to head downstream I took off. I was flying, positively racing. The landmarks that had taken an eternity to reach flew by. There was a small island that shot past to my right and then I made a turn back upstream to the finish. Again I thrashed against the current. Eventually strong arms and a firm grip reached down and dragged me from what seemed like the raging torrent, my nemesis, the placid River Thames, onto the landing stage. It was over, the nightmare had ended. I looked down at my watch, some 42 minutes.

Linds was waiting there, 'I think I'm last' I spluttered, downcast as I ran forward. 'No.' she re-assured me, 'There are a few further back'. Small consolation.

It was great to see her familiar face as, with a giddy head, I stumbled out of purgatory towards my faithful lilac steed. She ran the 200 yards with me to the entrance to transition. Grandma waved as I went past. I ran to my bike, towelled off the worst of the water and pulled on my vest. Luxury of luxuries, I strapped on my heart rate monitor (I don't bother these days). I then dried my feet, pulled on my socks and cycling shoes, put my helmet and glasses on, grabbed my bike and made a dash for the bike exit. Not the quickest or smoothest transition; it certainly wasn't going to win me races. I guessed I would learn as I went along. I mounted my bike, a few pushes on the pedals and I was off. The fun began. I like cycling. It has always been my favourite sport. It was a lovely sunny day by now and there wasn't a breath of wind. Perfect. The road was super smooth out of Windsor.

'Head down, let's go.'

After a little roundabout there was a long straight out of town. The roads were still quiet and as I was so far back in the field, I was in no danger of drafting. Drafting is a heinous crime in non-elite triathlon. It is tantamount to taking drugs or concealing a small motor to power your back wheel. No fear of that today. I pedalled on. Looking down at my speedometer, I was averaging 21 to 22 miles per hour. For some these speeds are slow; for me, I was cooking on gas. 'Be cautious,' I thought, and then 'to hell with it, I have got so far to catch up. Let's see how long it lasts'.

I went round a big roundabout and then another long straight into the country. At the top of the course the route crossed over the motorway and then the undulations began. It was getting hotter and I was drinking quickly. I should have taken two bottles out. Just keep riding. I watched the miles roll by, my speed was still good. Over halfway and the course was still undulating. Eventually I got to the long drag up to the turn point. I say eventually, but I was loving the bike ride. I flew past people who had exited ahead of me in the swim. From the turn point we were on the way back into Windsor. At about 21 miles the Castle came into view and then a great descent into town. We were racing now and the route felt really good, with some technical stuff through corners and roundabouts. In a way I was disappointed to see the town centre and the transition area. The ride came round the back of transition and suddenly I was dismounting. I had been going for about 2 hours by this stage.

From dismounting I pushed my legs into a run and there I was, back at my racking spot, pulling my helmet off, tearing off my shoes and tying the laces of my trainers. Again a reflex reaction propelled me forward into the run. And boy, did that feel weird. Jelly legs. Going from a bike ride straight into a run. If you have never done it, try it. Go on and give it a go.

The 6 mile run course was a star shaped three lap loop around Windsor city centre. The first leg was up the hill in front of the castle and then back down. The second was along the flat, round a cone and back. The third was over the river, down a street and back. Then the fourth took you toward the finish and then cruelly turned you back out onto the next lap, clutching nothing but an elastic band to show you had completed a lap and the hollow thought that you had to do it two more times. I got round once and found it hard going. I kept on pushing myself, up the hill, out to the cone, over the bridge, got my next elastic band. Actually it didn't seem that long. I was racing, I was overtaking people. Admittedly some were overtaking me too.

The elite men, who'd started 45 minutes after my group's start, caught me on the run. I guess I should have been pleased I'd held them off for so long. With my heart rate monitor on, I was keeping my heart rate between 164 and 172 beats per minute. Then, on the last lap of the run, I had a bit of a fright as the monitor started beeping at me and the display showed 200 beats per minute. What, was this it? The premature heart attack? Then as one of the elite men disappeared over the horizon and my heart settled down to a steady 170, I realised it wasn't me who should be worried. I was amazed that after racing a mile in the water and 25 miles over the bike course, he was still able to maintain 200 BMP. Is that good for you?

Up the hill, this was the last lap, round the cone, almost there, over the bridge, getting close, start to open up, make some places. By the finish I was going for it and then I was over the line.

My first Olympic Triathlon. I felt a little rough, a little giddy, quite light headed all in all. 2 hours and 48 minutes. My legs were burning from my sprint finish. There was some drink to hand so I stood by the dispenser and helped myself. As the lactic acid subsided I felt pleased with what I had done. I'd completed my first Olympic distance race. Okay it wasn't the perfect start but it *was* a start.

With the exception of my swim, I had raced. At last I could be proud of my BTA licence. What was more, I was almost interviewed by Sky Sports. Well, they interviewed the guy standing next to me at the finish. So close, the moment where I would prove my worth to Nike, but then maybe Sky thought their viewers would be more interested in hearing from Andrew Johns, one of the GB athletes. He had just won his place on the Sydney Olympics 2000 team, a momentous achievement given that this would be the first time triathlon featured in the Olympics. He'd qualified by winning in under 2 hours. I suspect my time of 2 hours 48 minutes didn't even warrant a derisory snort from the selectors. I think they'd packed up and gone long before I lunged over the line.

Linds found me and gave me a kiss. We went to find Grandma who was grinning from ear to ear, proud as punch. So was I. The sun was lovely and warm. What a great day. I changed into dry clothes and started to feel even better. We got my bike out of the transition area and had another look around the Expo. We perused a few tents and then I saw the bargain of the century. There was a really professional looking triathlon bike, dramatically reduced in price, made by Quintana Roo. Even the name sounded hardcore. With a black frame, deep rimmed grey wheels, super slick tyres, a high seat post, low handlebars and the sporting de rigueur accessory, aerobars with gear shifters on the ends, this bike was all I had dreamed of. No longer would I feel deep shame as I wheeled my weapon into transition. I had a chat with the guy on the stand to find out why it was reduced. 'Last years' colours' he assured me. Great. I wasn't fussy. Anything to replace my lilac penny farthing. I tried it out, had a brief chat with Linds about being committed to triathlon, and how I really needed a new bike, pulled out my credit card and bought the thing there and then. It would take two weeks to arrive. Great. My first race and a brand new bike. At that moment I felt life was great.

Windsor was a good day. I had grown a little in confidence and experience. But there was still a niggle.

2.4 miles, 112 miles and 26.2 miles....

Chapter 6

Post Race Blues

It was funny. There I was a week after Windsor and all I wanted to do was race again. I'd got the bug. It was some feeling. There were strong emotions before, during and after the event. Fear, nerves, pain and elation. I sat in work that week and all I could think about was racing again. All the other stuff seemed a little black and white in comparison. I had to feed my desire. Virtually the day after, I sent off for details of other races. It was like a drug. I'd also became obsessed with the arrival of my new bike.

All in all, despite my high spirits, my result at Windsor wasn't great. If anything, it confirmed my novice status. My swim time was a bit of a joke. I had been convinced, despite Linds' reassurance as I came out of the water, that I was last. The split on the Internet proved I wasn't. But still, 42 minutes. I had to improve on that. The lead male in my wave leapt out after only 18 minutes. 18 minutes, what was he doing, water-skiing?

On the other hand I had loved the bike. I was so over the moon when I calculated that I'd averaged 20.5 miles per hour over the course on the lilac mule. I'd had a real little race out there. Even the run wasn't going to break any records but it was a respectable time. I'd kept my head down and continued to race.

And now I had post race blues. There I was, back at work, contemplating what it must be like to be a professional athlete. I reasoned it couldn't be an easy life, just hard work, a world of pain and supreme pressure where your heart rate is constantly around 200 beats per minute. The training must be mind numbing. The racing must be crushing and the risk of losing form and dropping back must be immense. I tried to console myself; it couldn't be all tans and jolly training sessions in the south of France. I continued to daydream at my desk. It was a busy day.

Post race blues, watch 'em. That's all I'll say. It's very easy to slip into 'woe is me'. As I stared into space my world turned from stereo to mono. The truth is, I thought I would love to be a pro. It sure as hell would beat sitting in an office between the hours of 8am and 6pm, Monday to Friday, with the sands of time slipping through the hourglass. 'Woe is me'. How long will I get? 80 years if I'm lucky. How long will I spend working? Probably about 45 of them. I couldn't think about it.

Ah, the amateur philosopher. Was there any consolation? No, just enjoy what you do and make life as intense an experience as possible. For me Windsor was one of those intense moments and I wanted more. Working as hard as ever, I sat there with the wonders of modern technology at my fingertips, gazing at my results. I had my copy of 220 in front of me, with the events for the year listed. That day I sent off two entries. One for Milton Keynes Olympic Triathlon at the end of July and the other for a sprint race in Nottingham at the beginning of August. I decided to enter Brighton Olympic distance in early September and, barring injury, the Ballbuster Duathlon in November. I was contemplating doing the London Olympic Triathlon but I wasn't so sure. There was a marathon in Kingston on the 8th October and I really fancied pounding out another 26.2 miler before the winter. Oh yeah, and I shouldn't forget I had told the whole world I was going to do an Ironman. Nothing like peer pressure to strengthen the resolve.

It was a month after my revelation in the garden and I was pulling together a plan. I'd already figured out that I needed to maintain my fitness throughout the winter, something I had always found hard. Maybe it was something to do with motivation. The truth was, I was a fair weather athlete. I liked the warmth, I liked the sun. I knew that what I needed to do was buy some warm clothes, get an over jacket, some long tights and gloves. On the banks of the Thames at Windsor my passion had been rekindled. I needed to get my 'Ironman – Finisher' T-shirt.

I looked at my training. How was I mentally and physically after Windsor? Mentally I'd felt great. I'd felt motivated and confident that I could improve on my 2 hours 48 minutes. I had lost my fear, despite my atrocious performance, of open water swimming. I knew that the next time I was in a river I just had to swim as close to the bank as possible. The cycling I was comfortable with, especially with my new bike coming. I just needed to build up my distance. Ironically, although it didn't feel like it, running was probably my strongest discipline. Again, as with cycling, I just needed to build up the distance. I also figured the key to it all was staying injury free. I knew endurance came from continual training. The more frequently I was injured, the less I would be able to train. I needed to avoid injury.

However, despite this mental elation, I felt physically knackered. Due to work commitments, I didn't train the following Monday or Tuesday. This actually turned out to be a blessing as I had a few niggles when I woke on the Monday following the race. A stiff neck, a twinge in the hamstring and a dull stiffness in the lower back. I wanted to train but, despite my eagerness, I couldn't. And I would definitely recommend this shake down to anyone. By the time I came to train again, the troubles had gone. I shouldn't have rushed into it and fortunately I couldn't. As it turned out, even on the Wednesday I didn't train. The wind was blowing a steady 35 – 40 miles per hour so it was time to dust down the windsurfing gear and go out for a quick blast on the lake. Again this break did me far more good than harm. Thursday was my first training session.

I did a short run of 5 miles. I started off at a steady pace and cruised around my familiar, if you like, default course. I then met Neil and we did some weights at the gym. A gentle reintroduction you might think. I then went through to the pool and swam 750 metres. Foolish maybe, but it was fun. At this stage, that seemed a lot. My horizons were soon to be extended.

Chapter 7

Obsession

It was now almost four weeks on from Windsor. The summer was going by. I had gone through June and early July, the best time of year and I was learning loads. When I look back, I was learning about triathlon, endurance training and, more importantly, about myself.

I was enjoying the regular training and the motivation caused by the fact that there was something I was working towards. The training was unstructured, but more consistent than I had ever managed before. Typically, I'd train between four to six days per week. I felt fitter than I had ever felt before. My next challenge would be the local Olympic distance race in Milton Keynes. The only thing was, we had our summer holiday a fortnight before the race.

It was a great holiday. Linds and I went to Tarifa in southern Spain. Tarifa is one of the Meccas of the windsurfing world. It is billed as one of the windiest places in Europe. As an aside, it is supposed to have the highest suicide rate in Europe because the wind drives people insane. It was a great break and even on holiday I learned a thing or two.

The Milton Keynes Triathlon was only two weeks beyond the holiday and I couldn't let the training go whilst we were away so, as soon as we got there, despite the windsurfing schedule, I made a conscious effort to run. I did 11 miles on the first evening. It was great. The heat, the sun, this was real training. I also found a mountain bike centre and hired a bike virtually every day. Without my realising it, I was giving up one sport and becoming obsessed with another.

A typical day in Tarifa involved getting up, having a leisurely breakfast, then heading to the beach. The local wind didn't kick in until 2pm. By about 11am, 45 minutes into my book, I'd be bored of reading. I'd grab the car keys and head down to the mountain bike centre. I'd do an hour's circuit on the mountain bike, always trying to beat my previous time, then head back to the beach. We'd have lunch, grab a board and windsurf for 2 to 3 hours. I'd judge how successful the day had been by how long we'd spent outdoors. Linds and I weren't complete saints to the cause. We found a great bar that sold jugs of Marguerites (no, we didn't enquire as to whether they did them by the glass) where we managed to while away many drunken hours. It was a fab holiday. I even swam a couple of times. Okay, maybe once. But I reasoned my windsurfing ability ensured I swam a lot.

One of the things that struck me whilst I was out there was that diet is everything. I was a vegetarian at the time and had been since I was eleven years old. I always ate loads, but I didn't eat carefully. It wasn't until we met a physiotherapist in Tarifa and got chatting about training that I considered the possibility of lacking iron in my diet. He recommended I start taking iron supplements. Good advice, I thought, so I tried when we got home. I couldn't believe the difference. It turned out that a lack of red meat and other iron sources in my diet were causing an iron deficiency and therefore limiting the ability of my blood to carry oxygen. Before I started taking supplements I couldn't work out why I was so fatigued by day three to four after a rest day and didn't seem to be making a speedy recovery. Days five and six would always be a physical and motivational struggle. I started taking iron supplements and suddenly I could train six days in a row no problem. I was learning there was more to training than I'd thought.

The second tough lesson I learned was don't stop swimming. We got back from Tarifa and, true to form, within 30 minutes of putting the bags down in the front hall, I was in the car and heading to the gym. I did a weight session to flex my outrageous, but quickly peeling tan, had a quick strut round the pool and then dropped into the water.

I did my usual up, down, up, down, 4 lengths. It wasn't normally this hard. I turned to start my fifth, up to the top, turn and on to the sixth. What was going on with my arms? After seven and eight I thought, I'll do two more and then I need to stop. I had swum 250 metres and I needed a break. Talk about shattering my confidence. What had happened to my swimming? Milton Keynes Triathlon was two weeks away. Disillusioned, I struggled on, up and down. I had to split my remaining 50 lengths into 5 ten length sessions. Did I feel down? I vowed never to slacken my swimming off again. A vow I have often broken, incidentally.

There were a couple of other things I picked up on holiday. In the States they call Olympic distance races (remember by now this distance was my *piece de la resistance* at dinner parties) the 'short' course. The wind was taken out of my sails with that one. Okay, so the Olympic *is* a shorter course, but please don't rub it in. What's more, when you're out and you mention you're a triathlete, people automatically feel sorry for your wife. Okay, I already felt guilty.

Finally, with a week and a half to go to Milton Keynes, my new bike arrived. My new steed, a brand new black Quintana Roo Kilo. What I lacked in ability I would make up for by throwing money at it. Okay, so it was a bit naughty. The guys on the stand must have thought Christmas had come early. I had ridden it 300 metres in the transition area and out came the credit card. Sucker? I hoped not.

'Seven to ten days sir, we hand build it and courier it to you.'

Of course I needed to buy accessories for it. In truth, when everything was on it, the weight felt almost double. What did I get? Speedometer (of course), bottle cages (x 2, the seat post double bottle cage would have to come later. I could hardly wait), saddle bag (not a big one for a picnic, but a compact and lightweight one), 2 inner tubes, tyre leavers, light weight pump and track pump (you know, the one where you put your feet on it, then plunge down as if you're setting off dynamite. Just as an aside, the pressure gauge these come with is very useful). I stopped myself buying a new set of shoes and pedals.

Seven to ten days. Hmmm, let's just say the bike eventually arrived. There were many calls. I was getting sick of waiting. Sad I know, but in my mind this bike was the bollocks, it would make me a triathlete.

Eventually the box arrived at work. I could hardly contain myself. The afternoon dragged and as soon as the clock hit 5pm, I fled the office and headed to Neil's. I possessed all the mechanical savvy of a monkey, whereas Neil, my trusty handyman, would have her together in no time and we could then head out to christen her. We opened the box and there she was gleaming, half built. All we had to do was clip on the wheels, fasten the seat post, attach the handlebars to the front forks and transfer the pedals from my lilac steed. What could be simpler? Oh, the frustration that night. We spent all evening trying to get the bloody thing sorted. Neil and I were cursing, sweat dripping from our chins.

Why make it so complex? Attaching the handlebars mystified us, a master safe cracker would have struggled to unravel the mysteries of the 'stem' and could we loosen the pedals from my Peugeot? To avenge itself for my treachery, my faithfully abandoned bike of old wouldn't relinquish them to us. Two hours later, both of us feeling very harassed, we gave up. The Roo remained unchristened. I was tearing my hair out.

It was quite an evening. A deal was falling through at work so I was taking calls, sweat running off me, hands covered in grease, not really giving a monkey's about the deal. I just wanted to ride my black stealth machine. We eventually went for a ride, leaving the Roo in Neil's garage and me riding the old lilac penny farthing. I had waited weeks for this bike. Now it was here, it was about as useful to me as ice cubes are to Eskimos.

After our ride I packed the bike into the car and drove home. The deal was still falling through. Who cared? I carried on taking calls from work and the client. It was going to be a late night, so as I waited for calls I got the Roo out again and tried to fix the pedal situation. The pedals on the Peugeot still wouldn't budge. I guess this was the bike's revenge for my lack of loyalty to a companion that had served me well for a decade. Obviously I didn't see this at the time, just my near useless new black stealth machine.

By nightfall I was getting desperate and transferred my clipless pedals (my SPDs) from my mountain bike. Eventually, at 12.30am (yes the dark 12.30 in the middle of the night) after much swearing and cursing, I rode around the estate where we lived until 1am. How sad. I must have looked a real state. I was obsessed, probably quite unstable.

First thoughts, was I pleased? Not as much as I should have been. Was I worried? Yes. My back really hurt. This wasn't fair. I had just shelled out £1,200 and the bike was hurting me. No, no, no. Things weren't going right. I had to find a solution. It took me the best part of the next six months to get the Roo comfortable and after all that I ended up with a new bike anyway, although that wasn't because it was uncomfortable. That story comes later.

'If you turn the stem upside down, it will give you an extra centimetre,' Dick at my local bike shop, Phil Corley's, advised me the next day. The stem, for the benefit of the non-technical amongst us, is the bit that goes from the handlebars across to the tube up from the forks. Needless to say we figured it out and the extra centimetre made some difference.

I made a few other changes. I wasn't sure about the whole concept of having the gear shifters at the end of the aerobars. Therefore I had asked for the shop to put drop handlebars on the bike and fit combined gear shifters and brakes, before it was sent to me.

At this stage you have to be thinking I was a complete idiot, about as technically competent as a bronze age man who has barely grasped the concept of flint and fire. With my level of technical expertise I probably would have argued against the concept of the wheel. Basically, if that's your conclusion, you've got it in one.

Anyway, they finished the Roo with clip on aerobars, normal drop handlebars and STD shifters. I hoped this would give a more comfortable riding position. I knew the proof would be in the pudding so the next evening I took it out properly for the first time. Oh yeah. I rode like a man possessed. I found that riding on the aerobars was an aggressive riding position, but in actual fact was surprisingly comfortable. I also estimated that it added an extra two to three miles per hour to my average speed. I was delighted. I knew I had a really good bike. I was chuffed.

Another hot little tip. Speedometers are hard to fit to aerobars. Don't despair. You get Speedometer mounts that attach to your stem and are turned through 90 degrees from the normal handlebar ones. Mine cost me £2.99. Well worth it. Anyway, best stop boring you with all this technical stuff.

The bike was ready and I had a race to look forward to the following week. Summer had truly arrived. It was warm, windless. Triathlon was great.

There was also a plan forming for the Ironman.

Chapter 8

The Plan

There I was, with my new, shiny, black bike with aerobars, training hard. I had a full race calendar. Hell I was even starting to mistake myself for a triathlete. But something wasn't quite right. August was fast approaching and I knew there was something I had to do. It was constantly on my mind, like the sword of Damocles hanging over me. I knew I had to enter one. 'One' being an Ironman.

Despite my recent success at Windsor, I felt it best not get too excited. Coming 659th overall had hardly rocked the triathlon world and third from last in my wave exiting the swim had hardly sent the sporting press chattering 'the saviour of triathlon is here'.

An Ironman seemed massive. I looked at the Internet every day. I read the descriptions, poured over the maps and memorised the rules. There were two rules that really stood out:

From the run section; *'No form of locomotion other than running, walking or crawling is allowed'*. Crawling? Running, walking or *crawling*? What was I getting myself into?

From the description of the transition from bike to run; *'Athletes requiring IV fluids at this point in the race will not be allowed to continue'*. Intravenous fluids. It was mind numbing.

These two rules alone sum up Ironman. I had to enter, there was a momentum building up inside me. There was doubt, but that seduced me further. This would be the greatest challenge of my life. It seemed massive. I would break it down. By Christmas I would need to be able to swim 2.4 miles front crawl. Christmas seemed a long way off, it sounded easy. Within the next three months I needed to build up to 1.5 miles and then 2 miles by November, beginning or end I wasn't sure although I had a feeling it would be the end. If I could do 2.4 miles by Christmas, I would be happy.

As I've mentioned there are also time limits so I needed to be able to complete the swim course in 2 hours 20 minutes. I reckoned from there, with enough fluids and fuel, I could turn out 112 miles on the bike. Again with the time limit, there would be a 10 hour cut off from the start gun. Even if I took the maximum time on the swim, this left me with 7 hours 40 minutes for the bike course. But whichever way I looked at it, the marathon filled me with dread. 26.2 miles. I just didn't know.

Another rule; *'The marathon course will close officially at 12:00 midnight. All athletes still on the course past 12:00 midnight will be offered a ride to the transition area.'*

Always a comfort to know.

Chapter 9

The Inaugural Flight Of The Roo

I was tooled up. I was ready to win this thing. I had my new Roo and I was very excited about racing Milton Keynes Triathlon, my second Olympic distance. The dreams ran in my mind. Damage limitation on the swim, get out of the water, on to the bike. How would the field stay with me and my new bike? My Roo. My black stealth machine. Come off the bike, obviously leading the pack, with a strong run. This would be my break through into the UK and World Triathlon rankings. Sky, you'd better be ready to interview me this time. You missed your chance at Windsor. These were the daydreams that swirled around my head as I drove to registration.

Milton Keynes Triathlon was a great race. The swim was in Emberton Lake so there was no raging, polluted torrent to contend with. I had cycled the bike route the week before. Busy roads but quite manageable. And finally the run, three flat circuits of the lake. I had no real illusions about winning but this was a chance to vanquish the demons of Windsor.

Registration was much easier than Windsor. Just a tent in a field. T-shirt selection was easy. My 'No Excuses' Windsor Triathlon, long sleeved T-Shirt. Hell no one there knew I had come 659th and was no less than 3rd last out of the swim in my age group. Okay, so I wasn't Mister Super Cool. I still had the nerves, but it wasn't as bad as Windsor.

Again, stupidly, I wasn't content racing anonymously. I'd invited my mum and dad to watch this time. The pressure was on. After registration I went back home, got my stuff ready and prepared for battle the following day. I even slept. Funny how you get familiar with the routine. However, the alarm was still a shock the next morning. I got up and had breakfast quietly. No loyalty from Linds about seeing the start this time. She was the seasoned pro spectator and therefore harboured no illusions about me having a breath-taking swim.

I went through the now familiar routine of wake, drink tea, eat cereal bars, drink more tea, get the stomach going. Shave, shower and go to the loo as many times as possible. All done, I drove down to the start at Emberton Park. Now, I thoroughly recommend this race. The organisation was very good. There was a nice, friendly, non-intimidating atmosphere in the start area. That isn't to say other races aren't like this, but Milton Keynes Triathlon was done very well. I racked the Roo and was very excited about seeing how she would go. Two bottles of drink adorned the frame. I arranged my carefully selected clothes and accessories; cycle shoes, running socks turned inside out, trainers unlaced, talcum powder sprinkled lightly over all footwear (to help dry the feet after the swim) and vest with numbers. Again, I wore my cycling shorts under my shortie wetsuit.

I had a little jog around to warm the muscles, pulled on my wetsuit shortie and went down to the start. By now the nerves had well and truly kicked in. I lowered myself into the water with 10 minutes to the gun, to have a good splash back and forth. The water was about as clear as Brogborough, but at least it wasn't trying to wash me out to sea. With all my racing experience I had decided to get stuck in at the swim start, so positioned myself towards the front of the pack. As it was an anti-clockwise swim, I decided the right side of the pack would be more advantageous, my logic being that I wouldn't get crushed on the inside on the turn buoys. I knew I could go the distance but could I improve on my time?

The gun went off. It was bedlam. The space that I had so carefully selected for myself a few seconds beforehand disappeared in a seething mass of neoprene and white water. Two ways to play it; panic and drown, or get stuck in. I got stuck in, being mindful of not getting kicked in the face. I kicked rigorously to ward anyone off swimming right over me. I puffed my chest out and went at it like a Mississippi steamboat. My position in the pack, out to the right, proved to be over-cautious. I could only breathe to the right and therefore see to the right. Rather than taking guidance from those around me, well to my right, I found myself in open water, at least to one side of me. Forced to take my own sightings, I zigzagged my way up the course. Round one buoy, and the next, and then onto the next. This was much better than Windsor. Although black neoprene bodies were pulling away from me, the distance was slipping by much quicker. Pretty soon I was on the last leg and could see the pull out point.

Hooray, as my feet touched the muddy lake bottom, I could feel the lightness course through me. To my black shiny stealth machine. Strong arms reached down and helped me. Light-headed, I half-stumbled, half-ran through to the transition area. There were Linds, Mum and Dad cheering me on and wishing me well. Linds said something like 'only two-thirds down in the swim'. To anyone else this could have made them stop. To me, it was like sweet, sweet music.

My transition was still appalling. I towelled off. Yes, I know, as I write this my cheeks redden with shame. In my defence, it wasn't a full rub down, but more of a light swish to help me pull my vest on. My vest still snagged as I pulled it down. After a struggle and a wiggle I was dressed. I pulled on my helmet, placed my glasses on my nose and it was show time. I pulled the Roo from the rack and we were off.

I don't remember much of the bike section. I just put my head down and my little Roo flew. I lowered myself onto the aerobars and felt like the King of the World. The first lap disappeared. Mum, Dad and Linds had come out to the road to cheer me through. I waved from my aerobars, trying not to look too uncool now that I was a 'serious' cyclist. Off I went again. It was a blur but I was delighted with the Roo. Definitely a good buy. I was really enjoying this. Again, as quickly as it started, I was heading into transition. In truth, I would rather have done another lap on the Roo, but the format was the format. I found my spot, racked the bike, helmet off, cycling shoes off. I was still in mountain-bike shoes. The shame. Actually they were more comfortable than my old race shoes. Again I lost valuable seconds tying my trainer laces. Then I was off, running out of transition.

Mmm, what a sensation that was. Jelly legs. The feeling went after two thirds of a mile and I got down to the serious business of seeing if I could win this race. Truth was, I was starting an impossible battle. The winner was crossing the line at pretty much the same time I was leaving transition. All I could do now was salvage pride. The three laps fell away quickly and before I knew where I was, I had finished.

I was delighted. My time was 2 hours and 22 minutes. Okay, I hadn't set the world on fire but it was a huge improvement. I had now done two Olympic distance races and the second time was far less intimidating than the first. This I would learn is a 'truism' of life and really why pushing yourself simply means the boundaries keep extending.

It was great seeing Mum and Dad at the finish. I think Dad was very proud. I have great respect for both the oldies and it was great to have their smiles and congratulations. It sounds odd, but doing them proud has always been important to me.

So what lessons had I learned here? I needed to get swimming lessons; I needed to sort my transitions out; I needed to buy an all-in-one racesuit that I could wear under my wetsuit and I needed to get some cleat/lace fasteners to speed up my bike–to-run transition. It was time to get aggressive and minimalistic. No more towelling down. The world of triathlon would never be the same. We packed up, went to Homebase, bought a water feature for the garden and installed it. Okay, the aggression would have to wait until Nottingham the following week.

Chapter 10

The Roo Really Flies

Well, the water feature was working splendidly. The cable powering the fountain was expertly buried under the lawn. The patio was complete. This was living on the edge. I was certain Pete Goss had exactly the same water feature setup enabling him to reflect on the perils of the high seas. I was sure that as he sat in his back garden contemplating the 'roaring forties', 'howling fifties' and 'screaming sixties' he was soothed by the trickle of water over small over-priced rocks.

Like the week following Windsor, the high from the racing in Milton Keynes had filled my daydreams from the Sunday night to the Friday evening. My legs had felt heavy again on the Monday, my shoulders stiff and the small of my back sore. Conscious that I had another race in seven days' time I really did very little during that week, just some short swims, runs and fun, cruising bike rides. By the Friday I felt recovered. Before we knew it Linds and I were packing up on the Saturday to head up to Holm Pier Point in Nottingham to race in the Super Sprints. The format was a 750 metre swim in the rowing lake, a 12 mile bike ride which comprised 4 laps of the lake, and a 3 mile run, again around the lake. The course sounded far from scintillating, but I was very excited and the word on my lips was 'aggression'.

I had booked a hotel in Nottingham and, after driving several laps of the road system around the city in ever decreasing circles, we found the salubrious joint. Okay, it wasn't the Hilton but there was a bed. We dumped our bags and headed off for registration. All this was starting to feel very easy, just like falling off a log. Now that I had a small collection of event T-shirts, the conundrum was which one to wear? I write this smugly but there was always the guy with the 'Lanzarote Finisher' T-shirt haunting my subconscious. But hey, he wasn't at Nottingham that day.

Aggressive, aggressive. Bare the teeth. How to speed up transition? I'd learned that the amount of time in transition makes quite an impact on the overall time. At the Expo I found myself an all-in-one racesuit. The reps on the stand were great and they let me take a handful of sizes to the toilets to try on. With my nose a little out of joint, I came back and paid for the extra-large. These triathletes must be skinny little rakes. I even bought a number belt. Grrr, I was feeling aggressive.

We went back to the 'Hilton' then headed out for a meal. I even had a few beers (aggressive *and* cocky) and watched a firework display over the River Trent. Did I sleep? You know, I did that night. One big plus for this Super Sprints format was that it was on a closed course, so the start times were much more civilised. My race started at 10.30am.

All in all I was fairly relaxed. I was hardly a veteran but I had all the gear. ('All the gear and no idea' maybe?) I had my Roo. I had my all-in-one racesuit and my number belt. Okay, I still looked a bit of a novice in my yellow and black windsurfing shortie and I was still using my mountain bike shoes, but all of a sudden I felt as if I blended in, not so much the new boy at school.

As my start time grew imminent, I had a quick run about, the same old warm up. I pulled on my shortie and lowered myself into the murky water. The inability to see my hand or my elbow held no fear for me now. The start was 100 metres from the entry point, therefore I had a good warm up as we all swam out. Now the funniest thing occurred here. People looked more worried than I did. A smile grew inside. It was nice not to feel like the novice anymore.

I positioned myself for the start, again towards the front (well, okay, in the middle of the pack and to the right). This time it was a clockwise course so I would follow the buoys. Bang. Off we went. A flurry of white water and neoprene. I was starting to enjoy this. The smile grew bigger. Racing was great. A straight drag up to the buoy and I was giving it everything. Round and down to the exit of the swim. Out of the water. What so soon? Sprints were great. Now to my bike. Off with the shortie and hey presto, I was ready to go. Helmet, glasses and shoes on, grab the bike, clatter to the mount line and go.

Now we were rocking. Long straight, down on the aerobars, long bend, short straight, long bend, long straight, up to the top end, around and suddenly a lap had fallen away. Focus on the next person, overtake. This was great fun. The 4 laps flew by. Linds said afterwards that she was so shocked to see me leave the bike-to-run transition, she thought I'd missed a lap. I was having real fun. Aggression. Again another quick transition and I was off on the run. For the first time ever I was really racing and my legs felt strong. I was just concentrating on the person ahead and trying to reel them in.

I was delighted with my race, finishing 18th out of 80. Suddenly I felt part of a tribe. Over the last three races I had learned loads about myself and my technique. I was grinning from ear to ear.

Chapter 11

A Journey Begins

My heart beat faster. The e-mail read;

'This message is automatically generated as a confirmation of your recent registration at Active.com. You have successfully been registered for the event below – Ironman Lake Placid'.

All of a sudden it was real. Life had the sound turned up. I could feel a ringing in my ears. I read the e-mail a couple of times. Had I entered or had I simply registered? Did I need to book our flights? At every turn the world of Ironman was shrouded in mystery. I wanted to enter a race. It filled me with dread but I wanted to get in. Now, was I registered or was I entered? What was going on?

This day was very vivid. A big step. There was a buzz. I had entered something really exciting and truly started my journey. All of a sudden, from the routineness of daily life, I felt alive. I felt high on the adrenaline. I had a purpose, a challenge, something that would really push me, stretch me, test me.

As the excitement subsided, I sobered to the distance, the effort, the commitment, the energy and the single-mindedness required. I made a quick calculation and drew up a spreadsheet showing the countdown. I was 350 days from the start of Ironman Lake Placid 2001 in the USA.

What did 'Registration' mean? Was I entered into Ironman Lake Placid?

Chapter 12

Back To School

It was late August 2000. Life was good and I was training hard. I'd smile to myself and make up little ditties; 'Take a long, deep drink from the fountain of life, and you'd better hope it's isotonic'.

It felt great. The worry was over. I had successfully entered Ironman Lake Placid. On reflection, entering the race had been simple. All I'd had to do was go onto Active.com, select the race, fill in my details, pay my money and 'Bob's your uncle', I was in. To be certain, I'd e-mailed the race organiser and the confirmation 10 hours later told me the bad news. 349 days to go. The clock was ticking. My knees were hurting. Hopefully just overdoing it. A bit too much running. I was learning so much, especially about swimming. Now, where should I start? Did I hate it? Did I love it? Hate? Love? Hate? Love? I wasn't really sure. At day 345, the jury was still out. I just had a niggle. Is it me or is swimming pointless? Was I doing enough? Definitely not.

Just to show you what an ill-disciplined athlete I was, this is how I was sharing time between the disciplines. I cycled probably about three times a week. On average I did between 25 and 40 miles per ride. I also ran about three times a week, on average between 5 and 10 miles per run. I liked these two disciplines. In fact I would even go as far to say that I positively loved them. Yes, they were a bit of an obsession.

Now swimming. How easy was it to miss a swimming session? The silence was deafening. How far was I swimming? My face coloured with shame. I was training for an event where I had to swim 2.4 miles. At day 345 I was doing one half-hour session and two 15 minute sessions a week. Shame, shame, shame. Swimming didn't come naturally to me. If you played the hot air balloon game with swimming, biking and running, the guy in his Speedos would be plummeting to terra firma pretty early on in the game. I would always do swimming last. It was my worst discipline and the one I seemed to make the least improvement in. At the time I wondered why.

Looking back, the reasons were quite obvious. One was technique and the other was the balance of my training. Which one is the easier to improve on? Ironically, the former. It was time to swallow my pride. I picked up the phone. Ring, ring.

'Hi Lisa, yeah, um, I am a triathlete and I'm looking for some swimming coaching. I need to improve my technique.'

It was like something out of Alcoholics Anonymous. I dropped the 'I am a triathlete' bit in to try and impress her. I wasn't sure, but I think I heard a yawn. The conversation continued.

'I don't think it's fitness because I can swim for ages. I think it's more technique.'

'Why's that?' she asked.

'Well to give you an idea, it takes me about 30 minutes to swim a mile.'

'It's definitely technique.' she replied.

Wow, tell it how it is. So after the juggling of diaries, we set the date, the moment of truth, the awful truth, to determine how bad my swimming really was.

The Ironman was not the only prompt. In my last two races, I'd come out of the water midway back in the pack, only to make up the time on the bike and the run. In the last race I'd finished 18th out of some 80 competitors. For a top ten finish my swimming had to improve.

'Hi, I'm Stuart,' I said shivering in my Speedos. Now what followed was pretty sobering. Probably my only saving grace was that I didn't drown, but it was pretty close. For all my humiliation, everything she told me was true.

'If you swim four lengths to start with, I'll watch your technique.'

I powered up and down, with the grace and style of an Olympic champion. I was like a dolphin. If she had thrown me a ball, I would have balanced it on my nose. If she had held up a hoop, I would have dived through it. This was not my normal swimming. She had to be impressed.

I came to a stop, somewhat breathless, maybe a little more than usual. Hell, I had put on a good show.

'Mmmmm,' she paused, 'you may want to consider using your legs.'

She gave me some exercises which involved pushing a float in front of me and kicking very hard from the hip. It made a big difference to my speed. This was easy.

'Now try using your arms with full leg kicks.'

Using my legs, I drove up the pool. Wow, I was almost planing. One length, two lengths. What speed. Two and half lengths. Oxygen levels dangerously low. Three, three and a half. I'd slowed down considerably. Four. Aggghhh, air. Breathless, I was gasping.

'What next?' I asked trying to regain some control of my breathing and holding tentatively to the shattered remnants of my pride.

'Well, let's have a look at your arm stroke.'

Basically it was too short. I needed to reach as far forward as possible. Then as my 'paddle' ('hand', for the laymen amongst us) came through the water, I needed to maximise the pull. Interestingly enough, it is not just your hand that acts as the paddle, but instead the whole of your forearm needs to be used to gain leverage. That made sense. To give Lisa credit, she was telling me exactly what I needed to know, and telling me in exactly the right way to get it through my thick skull.

She gave me an exercise which involved holding a float between my legs to neutralise them (hang on, a minute ago I wasn't kicking, now I am?) to practise my new power strokes.

I surged off. Inevitably I came to a grinding halt after two and a half lengths. I managed somehow through flaying, thrashing and splashing to 'drag' myself the final length and a half.

There was Lisa smiling. I had truly met my nemesis.

'Now we need to breathe on both sides.'

My heart sank. I had known this was coming. I had practised before the lesson knowing she would take me through this ritual humiliation. Resistance was futile. She had taken my money. Oh, to hell with it. Let's cap it all. I'd end up drowning halfway up this damn pool and she would have to rescue me. What a story she would have for the swim club. These triathletes, what a joke.

I pushed off. Breathe to the right, take a deep one, it could be a while before you taste that sweet air again. One, two, three, breathe to the left. No, take in a mouthful of water. One, two, three, breathe to the right. Ahhh, sweet air. One, two, three, mouthful of water to the left. I was slowly drowning. Again to the right, yes, some air. To the left, underwater cough.

You get the picture? The inevitable two and half lengths later, head up, oxygen debt, brain panic, starvation of air whilst going full out at front crawl, gasping, rasping. What had I done? 2.4 miles of this. Christ, I could barely swim 2.4 lengths.

The lesson blew me away. Before it I could swim 90 lengths no problem (okay, I admit I was barely using my legs). But now I was reduced to just under 3. What should I do? Everything Lisa told me was true. If I worked at all the things she'd highlighted, I'd undoubtedly improve my swimming speed and, more importantly, my efficiency. At the time, what she was asking me to do seemed impossible. I needed to fundamentally change my swimming style. I needed to go back to the very basics and start again. Looking back, it filled me with absolute fear. Even a week and a half after the lesson, I was still undecided about what to do. I knew eventually I would be able to swim properly. I would go back to basics and I would work hard in the pool. I would concentrate on the one discipline I enjoyed least.

I guess the challenge, the doubt and the application, was the very essence of my Ironman.

Chapter 13

Into The Unknown

It was still late August 2000 and time for some self-analysis of the would-be Ironman. There were 329 days to go to the start gun and I was 20 days into my training schedule. So how was I feeling at this point? Basically, I was paranoid and worried. One injury and I would never make it to the start line. Paranoid does not go far enough. My knees were no longer aching, but after running one evening I had developed a little hot spot on the inside of my foot just behind and to the side of my big toe. Getting injured wasn't my only source of anxiety. My swimming lesson had made me acutely aware of the fact that I needed to swim more if I was to improve. But I still hadn't managed to fall in love with swimming. Almost by default, I'd want to go out for a bike ride. I knew this would have to change and I'd need to become far more disciplined about scheduling in time for swimming. The biggest tragedy was that the nights were drawing in. Outdoor, after work cycling would only be possible for another week. The sun was setting earlier each day, and with the busy evening traffic, it sat at a dangerously blinding angle as I finished my rides. Winter was truly on its way. Out came the tights, jumpers, gloves, balaclava and overshoes. Winter, the dark, the cold; I hated them all. But I had my goal to aim for. Ironman Lake Placid, 29th July 2001.

It was funny really. After all the deliberation about which Ironman to do and the hours spent pouring over various websites looking for my 'easy' Ironman, in the end the choice of Lake Placid was quite spontaneous. I'd opened my newspaper to see an aerial photograph of a mass start, 1,500 people furiously swimming in Ironman Lake Placid 2000. It looked awesome. I'd turned on my PC, gone to the registration page, entered my details and that was that. Only after I'd paid my money and got my confirmation did I start to really look at the challenge that lay ahead.

I was doing my research, picking up anything I could glean on the event, adopting the old adage 'Proper planning and preparation prevents poor performance', I learned that Lake Placid is in New York state, to the west of Boston and just south of the Canadian border. The weather would be hot but due to the water temperature, wetsuits were still recommended for the swim. Now I didn't have a full wetsuit, but I did have my shortie. I needed to make a decision on this. I knew the swim began with a mass start and followed a two lap circuit. Once you completed the first circuit and reached the halfway point, you had to get out of the water and run down the beach, then get back into the water to start the second lap. This logically seemed like a great opportunity to take a breather in the race. Therefore, I liked the get in and out of the water scenario. Hell, this was a 140 mile race. The key would be pace. If I wanted to take stock after 1.2 miles, just try and stop me.

The swim seemed pretty logical, although maybe I would live to regret that conclusion. Having said that I did have some worries about it, the first one being about the distance. I rationalised that a strict training regime would sort that. Secondly, the unanswered full wetsuit versus shortie question. I needed to make that decision. Thirdly, early chaffing. That would be a job for my old friend Vaseline. Then there was the worry about my goggles filling with water. Just wear them nice and tight. I could always adjust them on the beach bit. And what about the group start with 1,800 competitors? (The organisers were going for an even bigger field in 2001). My strategy was simply to get out of the way. There would always be chance to catch up later. Finally, water disturbance and wind blown waves on my breathing side. It was paramount to feel comfortable breathing both ways. I quote Lisa, the goddess of swimming.

With that plan alone, I figured that I was going to enjoy the swim. Maybe I would live to regret that too.

Now the transition. After the second lap of the swim, I had to remember not to get back into the water. Only a fool would make that mistake, wouldn't they? Instead, I needed to run/walk/stagger 400 metres to the transition and changing area. Now this was where the uncertainty crept in. Despite the fact I had now completed two Olympic distance triathlons, I couldn't help but feel anxious about what lay ahead. The scale was overwhelming, the distances involved, the sheer number of competitors, the complexity of transitions. The questions in my mind were endless. How would I find my bike? Where would my cycling clothes be? What should I do with my wetsuit? And most importantly, what should I wear? Looking at the pictures of previous events on the web, a number of cyclists seemed to go out with cycling shirts rather than vests. What would the weather conditions be like? What about shorts? Should I wear an all-in-one racesuit on the swim or would there be good changing areas? The ideal would be to wear a pair of cycling shorts with full padding. Clothing. A lot needed to be answered.

How should I approach the bike? How should I set my bike up? I'd read an article written by a seasoned Ironman professional which said that your bike should be like a sofa. I think she was referring to being comfortable rather than actually cycling around with scatter cushions. I figured it was all very well setting the bike up to give Chris Boardman a run for his money over a 4 mile Tour Prologue, but it was another thing actually riding as comfortably and aerodynamically as possible for 112 miles, leaving yourself in a good enough state to set out on a 26.2 mile run at the end of it. My biggest concerns on the bike ride were backache and neckache. I carried an old rugby injury in two places in my spine and I needed to ensure the ride was comfortable. I continued to tweak my riding position. Getting the height of the seat and the handlebars right was a real art. The seat was supposedly a simple formula. Take a straight legged inside thigh measurement from your groin to your heel and multiply the measurement by 109%. The answer to this sum should be the distance from where you sit on your saddle to the pedal crank. Your leg should be slightly bent at the bottom of the pedal rotation and as you ride your hips shouldn't rock from side to side. The handlebar setting proved to be far more problematic, mainly due to peer pressure. The de rigueur setting for the hardcore seemed to be to get your handlebars as low as possible which supposedly made your body more aerodynamic. The only problem with this 'munching your front tyre' setup was that it was unbelievably uncomfortable for my neck, shoulders, back and, fundamentally, my balls. I personally prefer the 'sit up and beg' riding position. It was very comfortable on the spine and undoubtedly left me very fertile, but awarded me all the aerodynamic qualities of a double-decker bus, not to mention the ridicule of my peers. In the end, I settled on a halfway house. I set my handlebars at about the same height as my seat and sacrificed absolute speed and style, opting instead for comfort.

And then there were concerns involving food, drink and fuelling. There would be feedstations every 10 miles on the bike course. What would they stock? How much would I need to drink? Could I eat and ride at the same time? What about gearing? Would I need to have extra gears put on my bike? I knew there were two loops on the bike course with a long climb at the end of each loop. I would worry about that later. One could worry too much. I read the course route religiously to prepare mentally for the bike ride.

And then there was the transition from bike to run. In theory, I've got off my sofa and now feel compelled to run a marathon. Oh, what to wear? Pretty important again, as I figured I'd be out there for a while. All I really knew was I needed a good pair of clean socks and lots of Vaseline on the toes. How would I feel? How would I feed? What sort of pace would I go?

The questions were endless. All I was certain of was that it was going to be a *very* long day.

Chapter 14

The Perfect Taper

The training was going well, if a little tiring at times. I had certainly upped the intensity. In the final fortnight of August I was doing some big sessions. Over the course of one weekend I swam 1 mile and cycled 54, then the next day I ran 4 miles and cycled a further 41. In the final week I swam 2.4 miles, 150 lengths. I was really chuffed as that had been a goal for December. What a boost. It had been quite simple really. All I'd done was slow my speed and pace myself.

However, I was burning the candle at both ends and cramming in as much as possible. During the second weekend in August Neil and I had been to the Bulldog Bash, a motorcycle Hell's Angel Party, just outside Stratford-upon-Avon. We'd rolled up late on the Friday night on Neil's renovated Honda Goldwing. It was great. Like driving through the Gates of Hell. Then followed two late nights, with their fair share of booze and fast food. As if this wasn't enough, I'd been invited to the Charity Shield, Manchester United versus Chelsea, on the Sunday at Wembley. It was frantic. We packed up our tent surrounded by sleeping angels early on the Sunday and tore home, only to shower, change clothes and head down to London.

Then there was the following weekend. The Reading Music Festival. I went with Linds and a good friend Dave. Linds had very kindly agreed to drive so Dave and I had a free ticket to consume copious pints of lager and then proceed to mosh with Rage Against the Machine, Slipknot, Placebo and The Stereophonics. Perfect training for any would-be athlete! I was barely on my feet at the end. Linds (Gawd bless her) didn't get a sound out of either of us on the way home, save for the occasional incoherent mumble or snore.

Not ideal preparation for the events which were to follow. Not only did I have the Brighton Olympic Triathlon the following weekend, I had entered a sprint event at Spelthorne three weeks later, a marathon in Kingston during the first week of October, finishing the year with the 'Ballbuster' Duathlon in November (an 8 mile run, a 24 mile bike ride and a further 8 mile run up Box Hill in Surrey).

Something told me I wasn't getting the balance right. Easy to write, but difficult to achieve. It needed to be about training, recovering, having a life and enjoying myself. With the exception of recovery, I had been doing them all to excess.

With the rock and roll lifestyle of the Hell's Angels party and the Reading Festival only a week behind me, Brighton arrived. In truth, despite the bravado, I was pretty nervous. There were rumours of heavy seas. I knew from my windsurfing days that Brighton had an unforgiving shore break and I'd even seen footage of the top pros being humiliated in the angry seas. Well, in for a penny, in for a pound, I thought as I nervously watched the weather the week before. It looked good but even a light breeze could push up the waves.

Now for those who don't know it, Brighton is a great city. We drove down on the Saturday to register and catch up with an old University housemate, John. I was fairly relaxed about the whole registration bit by now. I'd packed considerably less than my cautious 'everything but the kitchen sink' days at Windsor. I'd got my kit down to; shortie wetsuit, all-in-one racesuit, helmet, Oakleys, socks (still), trainers, cycling bottles, number belt, Vaseline, baby oil and a few safety pins. It made everything much easier. I still left nothing to chance though and cross-checked everything religiously against the standard checklist I had put together. I figured there was nothing worse than arriving to find something missing.

Brighton is a great course for the spectator. The swim is a two lap 750 metre triangle, that is dependent upon whether the tide is either in or out. When it's out, the course is more of a run than a swim. As you come out of the water there is quite a distance to cover up the beach to a secure transition area and then out on the bike for multiple laps. It's a fast course, mainly along the seafront, but potentially boring for participants and open to misunderstandings, i.e. losing count of laps. I vowed I would be very careful to count my laps. To do this I put bits of tape on my handlebars and I would remove a strip each lap. I would also keep an eye on my speedometer.

Bike course complete and back into transition, it's then on with the trainers and off for the 6 mile run which comprised three laps of a circuit. Again, a fairly monotonous run. Just out and back along the front. See how professional I was getting, even reading the course profile.

So feeling familiar enough with the course and having racked my bike, we went off to meet John. It was a good night although I don't think he quite understood what I was up to. An early bed, alarm set and ready for racing?

Now Brighton has age group staggered starts like Windsor and, because it's a closed course, the start times of the later age groups are very civilised. My wave was off at 10.45am. Very civilised indeed. However, I'd read in the race briefing pack that once the first race had started you couldn't re-enter transition. Therefore once again we all suffered together. Well, all apart from Linds, who stayed in bed whilst I set up my transition. She waited patiently and composed for me to return and pick her up.

The luxury of getting there early is that you can see the other waves start. Brighton is great as you can stand on the front, on the raised section, and get a bird's eye view of the swim and transition area. I was encouraged to see that the tide was on the side of the athletes. As the first wave set off, the tide was so far out and the water so shallow that it was practically a run course. However, unfortunately for me, the tide was on its way in, so I didn't benefit from the sea's compassion.

Much to my relief, the sea was flat and calm and the sun was strong in a cloudless blue sky. As I watched events unfold, I decided I was going to enjoy this. My start time drew closer and my nerves started to build. As ever I fretted about the toilet arrangements, the good old pre-race dump – sorry to be so crude, but it's probably my biggest obsession before all races. With the undignified pre-race preparation out of the way, I pulled on my old shortie and headed down to the start. Despite my 'experience' I couldn't suppress the butterflies. So much for the big cool start. It was a new format for me this time with a beach start. Therefore I chose my spot in the middle and as the gun sounded I made a dash for open water and France. I smiled as I settled into my rhythm. I loved racing. The nerves, the scramble and now the work began. With the race certain to take me over two hours to complete, I quickly settled down to a comfortable, if not a little challenging, pace. There was a certain tranquillity and balance to it. Not too fast but by no means a slouch. A mile in the sea seemed a daunting prospect, but the first lap fell away relatively easily (well, it passed without incident). I hadn't lost as much time as usual, using Milton Keynes as a comparison. I was about two-thirds of the way down the field. Out on the beach, the irrepressible cheer from Linds penetrated my water-filled ears. I ran round the turnaround buoy on the beach then it was back out towards France. It's funny, I dreaded the swim, I dreaded swimming training, but despite all my bitching, when I actually swam I really enjoyed it. Round the first buoy again, along the top of the course, around the second buoy and what do you know, I was heading back to the beach and my waiting steed. Wow, now what was happening here? As I swam away from France towards the beach I actually started to accelerate and pull away from some of the folks around me. Hang on, I was in a swim race. Maybe Lisa wasn't just being rude but actually knew her stuff. Top tip, go and get swimming lessons.

Despite my incredulity at actually speeding up, there I was, back on the beach. Onto the carpet, long run up, over the miniature railway and into transition. Wetsuit off, shoes and socks on. Cautious of not racing with sand on the feet I had a bottle of water and a towel to hand. Too cautious. It's my Mum's influence really, she sees the danger in eating jelly. Every time I am in a dangerous situation I hear her voice warning me about a potential evil. Helmet on, mandatory Oakleys on, Roo off the rail and out to complete my laps. It was a delight being on the Roo and the laps fell away. However, for some reason I wasn't feeling super agile. I couldn't quite turn on the power. I seemed to lack my fourth gear. By the sixth lap I was dizzy with the laps. How many had I done? How many still to go? Even my tape pieces on the bars were bothering me. Still, I had my speedometer. The last two laps seemed to drag. Was it me or the format? The run provided the answer.

With a quickish transition and jellified legs, I ran off to start my 6 miles. Now, where I lacked a fourth gear on the bike, on the run it felt as if someone had hitched a caravan to my back. My feet were like lead. As I passed Linds on each lap I'd say 'I'm going to start my sprint soon'. The signal from the brain went to the legs and nothing happened. I couldn't turn it on. By the third lap I'd decided it wasn't going to be my day. No personal best today. So I plodded on, caravan in tow.

I finished in 2 hours and 30 minutes, 9 minutes slower than Milton

Keynes. On the run I had felt as if I was going backwards. All the training and I was getting worse. Why were my legs so heavy? Could it have something to do with the nine pints of lager, the mosh pit and Slipknot the previous Sunday and partying with Hell's Angels the weekend before that? Moderation would be a better strategy for the future.

Having said that, I really enjoyed Brighton. Lovely town, well-organised event, with a really friendly field. I was kicking myself for my somewhat wayward preparation. Oh well, Spelthorne in three weeks. That would be my chance to break into the pro ranks. Hope sprang eternal.

Chapter 15

One Year On

One year on from my baptism by fire and Spelthorne Sprint Triathlon had come round again. Here I was getting ready for a race in which I actually had some experience. I also had last year's T-shirt and a quiver of alternatives. One year on and a lot of water had passed under the proverbial bridge. Not that I was feeling cocky, well, maybe I was a little bit. This would draw a real line in the sand in terms of my progress over the last 12 months and I was extra excited as I had someone to share the build up with. Neil had believed my lies about triathlon being fun and signed up for his first race. Now I had to play it cool as he was absolutely bricking it.

Neil is one of the funniest people I know. We had windsurfed together for years. We both cycled and skied and shared the same interests. I had been Neil's 'bitch' on the back of his bike at the Bulldog Bash. Now he was lining up to take his first tentative steps in the world of triathlon. Neil is an active guy, but a hard drinking, hard smoking youth had left him a little short of racing experience and true to form, all the little demons in his mind were whipping the doubt into a frenzy.

Spelthorne is a race I thoroughly recommend for any novice triathlete. It is set in a leisure centre. The 400 metre swim is in the pool and the transition is in the tennis courts. Both the bike and run courses are flat. The start is a staggered time trial style, rather than the mass start. The other thing in its favour for me was that it was a fairly local race just off Junction 13 of the M25. Therefore with the two bikes on the back of the car, Neil, Linds and I set off early Sunday morning for Neil to bag his first triathlon and for me to see how far I had come in 12 months.

The weather was overcast, coolish, but dry. We arrived, registered, got our start times and set up our transition bits. The look on Neil's face reminded me of how I felt 12 months ago. To say he looked a little nervous would be generous. Obviously, now that I was playing the experienced veteran, I affected a little swagger. I don't think it helped Neil too much. But it created another good rule for me, like the old dating wisdom, want to pick up girls, go out with your ugly mate. Want to feel experienced at triathlons, take your mate who has never done one before.

Neil was starting before me and was looking very worried as we got to the poolside. I wished him luck and Linds and I stood by the pool to see him start. As he queued for his lane, shivering in his Speedos, he looked distinctly as if he wished he hadn't listened to me. As he lowered himself into the water, he shot me a hostile look. I hoped our friendship would endure this. I had so many DIY projects to do.

And he was off. I went outside so I could cheer him on from his transition. He came out pretty much on his predicted time. The scowl had transformed into a grimace and when he saw me the word he uttered began with a 'w'. Harsh, I felt. Obviously over the last seven minutes I had become the object of his spleen. Maybe our friendship wouldn't last.

Worried, I went off, did my warm up and duly lined up for my lane. Bang. I was off. I hoped that Neil would be alright. Up and down the lanes I went 16 times. It was actually a little pedestrian. Where was the rough and tumble of the group start? Where was the surge of adrenaline? As soon as the swim had started it seemed to be over and I was running to the tennis courts. Socks on, shoes on, helmet, sunglasses, off I headed, out on the Roo. Head down, start winding up the gears. I knew the course. I knew I could go over the distance. Along the Thames, back towards Spelthorne, smile for the camera, stop at the traffic lights (second year in a row I'd been stopped by the red light, unlucky). Back into transition, helmet off, shoes off, trainers on. Out on the run. As ever, for the first half mile my legs felt like jelly. I wondered whether I could catch Neil. As the jellied legs eased off, I started to stretch my stride. I pushed myself hard over those 3 miles and before I knew it, it was all over. I was breathless but felt I could do more, much more. Overall I was very pleased. I had pushed myself all the way. My transitions were smooth. I had known what to expect. I had raced. I had finished 11th.

Wow – wouldn't it have been great to finish in the top ten. Funny how you're never satisfied. Having said that, I was delighted. I had come a long way within the last 12 months. There was elation. I felt high. I had got off my backside and become something. All of a sudden I felt like a triathlete. Yes, I had all the gear, the Roo, the Giro helmet, the Oakleys, the all-in-one racesuit. But it was more than that. I didn't feel a fraud any more. I had seen something I felt was a challenge and I had gone beyond that challenge and it was really quite easy to do.

Back to reality, I wondered how Neil was? Brace, ready for the punch. And there he was in front of me grinning from ear-to-ear. We shook hands, smiled and although nothing soppy was said, I'm sure we felt the same inside.

Linds and I couldn't stop him talking on the way home. He was over the moon. We talked racing and bikes and running technique and nonsense. We didn't talk feelings. Men don't. But I was chuffed to see him so thrilled. I am sure it was the vanquishing of the things that hold you back. The realisation and completion of something that you think other people do because they are different or special.

Neil and I didn't talk about this, maybe these weren't his thoughts, maybe they were just mine. But I didn't think so. As we drove home, the heavens opened. Summer was truly over.

PART 2

Dressed Like An Eskimo

Chapter 16

Like A Hamster

Woe is me. It was October. The heady days of summer were long gone. The Ironman felt a long way off and motivation was low. The winter training schedule was pretty uninspiring, to say the least. I could only really get a decent cycle in at the weekends. If I started running at 6pm, it was dark within 30 minutes. Every week it was getting a little darker and a little colder.

I was staring down the barrel of five months without racing a triathlon and I felt pretty sorry for myself. I had really enjoyed my racing year. Spelthorne had been a great race to end the triathlon season on. I felt that coming 11th overall was the apex of my multi-sport career to date.

The demise of summer had come somewhat abruptly the week after Spelthorne. It was as if someone had turned the lights out, going from one week, riding out after work, to the next week where it was a case of 'Hey, where's my car parked, pass me the torch.' That was a shock.

I had to change my routine. All of a sudden swimming was a viable option, in fact an attractive option. For cycling I had a turbo trainer, although I loathed turbo training. Time stood still. I would start off all enthusiastic sitting on my bike in front of the TV or video and start peddling away, but somehow turbo training always seemed to make the earth slow on its axis.

How was I going to get through the next five months when I put turbo training in the same category as having my teeth pulled out? I was saved by the miracle of spinning classes. Whoever invented spinning classes at their gym was a genius, and one who I suspect came from a turbo training background. For those who don't know what spinning is, it's basically collective turbo training. Most gyms will have spinning classes, a semicircle of bikes with an instructor playing motivational music, telling you to sprint, climb and grind the gears. You adjust the resistance according to the gradient you want. I decided it was time to get along to spinning classes.

Now spinning for the non Ironman aspirant is nothing short of a great workout. But for me, oh no, a 45 minute class would never do. Not really the 'hard man' stuff I was looking for. All a bit too mainstream and dare I say it, normal. Don't get me wrong, I would bet money you'd never find Alan Titchmarsh in lycra standing up in the saddle for eight seconds and climbing for eight, 'Come on Titchmarsh, stop hiding those gears under the towel, more resistance, feel the burn.' But it was a bit pedestrian for me. I would spice it up therefore with either a swim beforehand (say 30 minutes) or a run afterwards. I resolved to spin two to three times a week and I would still be able to do a long ride at the weekends. The running wouldn't suffer really, as Milton Keynes had very well lit running routes. I just had to be braver and wrap up. The tingle was back. It was great planning to be abnormal.

Anyway, just in case I felt like slacking off, I had the Kingston Marathon in the third week of October and then the infamous Ballbuster duathlon in early November. No time for complacency.

The summer had gone so fast. All used up. Had I used it well? I think so. Any regrets? Spend more time with my wife, my truest friend, my most loyal supporter. I must step off the hamster wheel every once in a while.

Chapter 17

Marathon Running

The Kingston Marathon had come around. I had only ever raced one marathon before and here I was about to test the distance again. I knew from my limited experience that marathons are a long way. I knew the second half is longer than the first half. And I knew that marathon running is not fun running. It is a painful and humbling experience.

It had been another early Sunday morning start. Buoyed by his success at Spelthorne, Neil was running his first half-marathon so, both as nervous as each other, we piled into the car with our loyal supporters, Linds and Jackie, Neil's wife.

The week beforehand, the pressure had started to mount with the arrival of the race information pack. It stated 'There will be a cut off time. You must be on your last lap (18 miles completed) by 2 hours 40 minutes. Should you be outside this time you will be invited to retire'. What? Oh my God. Not only did I have the pressure of finishing in a good time, I could also be asked to retire. The shame. In the gleeful words of Neil, the new 'veteran' triathlete, 'What a story, asked to retire, oh how many times would we recount that one?' To which I responded, 'When are you going to take that Spelthorne T-shirt off?' After a quick calculation I worked out that 2 hours 40 minutes equated to 8 minutes 48 seconds per mile. Could I be slower than that? The greatest humiliation of my short Ironman life. Asked to retire from my second marathon.

But I was prepared. The previous night I had picked out my outfit carefully. I had opted for a Helly Hansen thin long-sleeved top, lycra shorts, thick walking socks and my Nike Air Max trainers. I felt I was tooled up and ready to go. I'd picked up a hot tip before the London Marathon which was to cover your toes in Vaseline. It works. I haven't lost a toenail or suffered a major blister since that day.

So there I was, my toes swimming in Vaseline, all ready to go. After the hustle and bustle of the London Marathon in 1999 and the tens of thousands of runners, Kingston was a quiet affair. As I jogged around the main shopping centre on that damp Sunday morning, it felt slightly more exclusive and exciting.

My previous best at London had been 3 hours and 34 minutes, and with a season of triathlons behind me, my daydreams had seduced me into thinking I could smash that. The reality was I didn't have the miles in my legs and my illusions of finishing in under 3 hours would evaporate without a trace. As the start got closer I made one final visit to the loo.

I had a quick stretch then found myself lining up with what looked like some very competent runners.

Bang went the gun, there was a chorus of cheers from the small crowd of loyal supporters and we were off on the serious business of covering 26.2 miles as quickly as our legs would carry us.

On paper it was a great course, flat as anything (apart from a cheeky little rise onto Kingston Bridge, ouch). It was three loops of a very scenic route, although by the end of the second lap I have to admit I wasn't taking in many of the sights. It was funny, but each lap seemed to get longer. My split times say it all. With the excitement of the start and the gun, I came out of the gate too quickly. For the first 2 miles my average time was 6 minutes 48 seconds per mile. Very fast for me. In fact, way too fast for me. At 13 miles I had slowed slightly to 7 minutes 21 seconds per mile. Over the second half of the run my splits were approximately 8 minutes 19 seconds per mile. I had gone from being the hare to being the tortoise. Had I started out too quickly? Yes, definitely. However good my first half was, my legs just didn't have the miles to do a quick second half. They just hurt. My knees ached, my quads felt like hot knives had been stuck into them and my hip flexors screamed with every step. At about 16 miles I was running low on sugar. Fortunately, my loyal supporter, Linds, was on hand with my own personal feedstations. Although if truth be known, she was quite distracted. Jackie and Linds were away with the fairies putting the world to rights half of the time and almost missed me on one occasion.

Mile 21 was my nadir. Now, I'm not prone to being a drama queen, but with legs on fire and the engine running on air I even considered crying as a release. It was madness really. The logical option would have been to stop. Amazingly, I had put myself voluntarily in this situation. Crazily, I had even paid money to do it. And in a heartbeat I could just retire and stop. It would have been that easy and that awful. No, I decided this pain was far easier than the thought of giving up.

I was slipping from a jog to a quick shuffle when I was saved by a couple who turned out to be triathletes (they're a good bunch). They came alongside, said 'hello' and proceeded to pull away. I slipped in behind and watched their feet and started to make conversation. Hell, whether they wanted conversation or not, I had someone to talk to. What a difference. Connection with the outside world. Reality, rather than the pain that was grinding me to an ignominious halt. It even turned out he had completed an Ironman. What could I say? Respect.

Suddenly the pain in my legs subsided and I felt better. I felt human. It filled me with strength and those final miles didn't appear so lonely or daunting. I felt positively fresh and the next 3 miles fell away. I was like a phoenix soaring from the ashes, and, having forgotten mile 21, I decided that at the 24 mile mark I would forge ahead alone for the line. In the words of the great marathon runner I was, 'I'm going to try and roll it out'. And there I rolled for a while. Boy, did those next miles hurt. The pain came back to the top of my legs. I gritted my teeth. My shoulders stiffened. I contorted my fingers into knots. My knees tightened and the knives stabbed back into my quads. But hey, I was 'rolling it out'. I ran/shuffled up to Kingston Bridge and cast a glance over my shoulder just to confirm the gulf I must have put between me and my triathlete buddies by now. Inevitably, despite my teeth grinding and my grimacing, they were only 20 metres behind me, happily chatting away. There was a lesson here. Something about balance, pace and feeling comfortable.

How did I feel at the finish? Oh boy, just great. Well, great, if you consider feeling nauseous and queasy as a sign of healthy living. After about 10 minutes, the pain started to subside. Just a feeling of dizziness, light-headedness and wanting to be sick. Oh so dramatic again. Running marathons is not fun running. However, my overall time was 3 hours 23 minutes 51 seconds, a new personal best, which gave me an average run split of 7 minutes 46 seconds. I have to admit I was pleased.

At the finish I had simple priorities. Drink, replace sugar, sit down, get warm clothes on. Get my event T-shirt. Try to make the limp look natural.

It was only 6 hours after the finish, when I was on my third bag of crisps, that I could start to admit I had really quite enjoyed it. Looking back on an overcast, damp day by the River Thames, it had been a long run. I couldn't imagine how I would cover the ground between the end of the bike course and the finish line on 29th July next year.

But I had knocked 11 minutes off my personal best. It had been a great day, although admittedly it was a funny way to spend a Sunday, locked in battle with myself.

Was I mentally imbalanced? Probably. Everything was focused on training or racing. I constantly needed to get my fix. I had become obsessed. If I was going to be late out of work and it looked like I would miss my session, I would actually get a sick feeling in the pit of my stomach. It was as if I was being cheated. Once I had trained, all the stress of the day would wash away. Weird really. A healthy addiction? I was Doctor Jekyll and Mr Hyde. If I didn't train two days in a row I'd get grumpy and restless. Linds could see it and would send me out.

This obsession caused problems with recovery. I knew I had to be careful after Kingston. I'd learned the hard way after the London Marathon when I had started running again too quickly. I had gone out whilst my knees and ankles were still inflamed and the consequent strain put my running on hold for four weeks. Therefore caution was my approach this time. I vowed not to run for a fortnight. My legs and muscles were stiff for a good part of the week following Kingston. I experienced swelling below the knees and my feet puffed up. But I couldn't just do nothing.

Two days after the marathon doing nothing was driving me up the wall. It was amazing how much training occupied and enriched my life. On the Wednesday I went for a swim and on the Thursday night I did a 45 minute spinning class. I swam again on Friday and went out on my bike at the weekend. My legs felt stiff and heavy but light spinning seemed to ease them off. Anyway, it did wonders for my fragile state of mind. The following week I followed a similar routine. My legs were still heavy, yup, two weeks later, but I just set my sights on the Ballbuster duathlon in early November.

I had settled into a routine and I had a good balance. Work, train, head home and see Linds. I was happy and enjoying myself. I felt fit and strong. I was over my winter training blues.

Most days I logged on to the Lake Placid Ironman website and most days I felt the tingle and excitement inside. The Ironman was there all the time. Not a day went by when I didn't think about it. It had a menacing presence.

Chapter 18

Busting My Balls

'The faint-hearted need not apply'.

Now if ever there was a race that lived up to its reputation, it was this one. The name said it all. Ballbuster. The infamous winter duathlon organised by Human Race.

The format was simple, an 8 mile run, followed by a 24 mile bike ride, followed by another 8 mile run. When you write it down it doesn't sound too bad. But then you lay it over Box Hill in Surrey, just off junction 9 of the M25, and it starts to get a little harder. Box Hill is an impressive fortress of a hill that rises menacingly out of the Surrey countryside. Literally, you are driving along towards Dorking, you go around a corner and suddenly there is this massive shoulder rising in front of you. The course is quite simple but the challenge lies in its bends, steepness and undulations. It's a legend.

As you start the climb, the angle of the road is deceptive. It doesn't look that steep, but I'm always shocked to find myself standing up in the pedals climbing in my lowest gear. Basically the route goes up the hill five times over five laps. The first is by foot, the next three are with your bike between your legs and the fifth back on your pins. Hence the name Ballbuster. What a winter race.

The last time I had entered it had beaten me. Like a fool, I'd rolled my ankle two weeks beforehand playing football in a 'friendly' at work. This year I sent my entry in early, determined to cross this fabled race off my 'to do' list. The race information pack came through two weeks before the event and as ever the nerves got even greater. The pack warned that this was a tough race, required the exertion level of a marathon and was not to be taken lightly. I smiled smugly as I read it. Then I thought about it and realised that I would be running 16 miles in total. That's a long way. The apprehension crept back.

Now if the course isn't tough enough on its own, there are also the weather conditions to contend with. 'The weather can be adverse' the pack warned. It concluded that care should be taken with the clothing selection on this one. 'Hypothermia has been known', the pack cautioned. Mmm, maybe this wouldn't be the walk in the park I had kidded myself into believing when I sent in my cheque during the heady warmth of summer.

In terms of a recce a few weeks before the race, a good friend and colleague, Nick, and I had diverted en route from an appointment and had driven the course. It had seemed a long way even in his car. I was starting to realise that this was probably going to be the toughest race I had done yet.

With all the hype and build up I was determined to bag the Ballbuster. But as the weeks grew nearer, a tickle in my throat moved to my chest and my head filled with cold. I felt crap, I was run down and miserable. Truth be known, I was pretty sure I was close to death. It was so bad that my coughing was waking me from my sleep. Racing would be silly. Everyone told me to forget it until next year. Sound advice really. With the Grim Reaper sharpening his scythe, this would probably be a wise one to miss. Good sense would prevail.

I don't think so. The Ballbuster had beaten me last year. I wasn't going to let it become the nemesis in my annual calendar. No, I would go, and that was that. But I really felt terrible. Even on the evening before race day I was still uncertain, but I packed the car anyway. I slept badly and as the alarm went off I still wasn't sure whether it was a good idea. But I got up and went through my morning routine. Drink tea, light breakfast, get the stomach working. My heart wasn't in it. I got in the car and headed south towards Box Hill. With the heating on full, I pulled into the National Trust car park feeling very sorry for myself.

And there in the half-light of a reluctant dawn I sat. It was bleak, raining, cold, grey and very windy. Autumn was in full swing, bare trees, leaves whipping around, still more night than day. So this was the Ballbuster. As the light grew and the car park slowly started to fill, so did a raw, exciting energy. There was an anticipation, expectation and nerves. People were a little wide-eyed. The wind tore through the trees and the rain fell in squalls. Here we were on the top of a hill about to embark on a race tougher than a marathon, in miserable winter conditions. This was life on the edge. As I dressed myself in my heated car, I had no doubt that the Ballbuster was everything the myth had made it out to be. And I had joined the brigade of nutters. Suddenly, I felt a lot better. I felt my eyes widen in wonder and excitement. I was glad I had come. I would go ahead with it.

That decided, I went to register. BTA licence in hand I walked out with my Ballbuster prize, a sweatshirt with 'Balls Busted' emblazoned across the chest and back. Subtle, but what a prize. There was a slight moment of panic as I found the National Trust loos locked and heard the devastating news that the guy with the keys couldn't be found. A few of the harder competitors went off to make like bears and relieve themselves in the woods. But for me, my resolve crumbled. Okay, so I could race with a cold, but to miss my final loo stop, now come on, wasn't that going a bit too far? Fortunately after a small number of us had calculated our chances of breaking the door in (I know, close to sacrilege, especially on a National Trust site) the key holder appeared. The necessary pre-race activities took place.

And there I was on a windswept hill, in a state of health that most people would have called in sick for, about to race. Not that sensible really. But fortunately I had Linds' common sense with me. To ensure she wasn't prematurely widowed, I had sincerely promised that I wouldn't race. I would just get round. What was more, I would wear all the warm clothes I could get on, really take care of myself. And finally, I would stop if it became too much. Well, at least I kept a quarter of the bargain.

I put on my racesuit, a vest, my winter-bib tights, a short sleeved cycle shirt and a long sleeved cycle shirt. I would wear these items for the first run. Then I planned to put my waterproof jacket on for the bike ride and see how I felt on the last run. With all these layers my biggest risks were dehydration and heat exhaustion rather than exposure.

By the start time the day was as bright as it was going to get. After a quick race briefing, we lined up. The gun went off and the charge began. The front group flew away, across the field, on to the road. Within minutes there was already a long line stretching out ahead. Pace, steady, take it easy, I coached myself. People were pulling away. Remember you've got a cold, it's just a training race.

Oh, bollocks to it. I quickened my pace and went for it. People stopped passing me and I started to claw back a few places. I just concentrated on who was ahead and who was beside me. Looking back on the Ballbuster I get flashes of leafy lanes, wet corners, muddy verges, old flint houses and walls. But in truth, at the time it was all a blur. It was tough.

The first run went pretty quickly. The Hill itself was soul destroying, energy zapping, long, and relentless. But before long I made it back to transition. With tight legs, I pulled on my jacket, helmet, glasses and gloves, then half-jogging, half-running, headed across the field with my bike and on to the road. 24 gruelling miles stretched ahead of me.

Cautious as ever, my promise to Linds in my head, I was making sure I drank plenty of fluids, staying warm and keeping my fuel up. I think it was on my second lap of the bike when the pros went flying past. As they whipped past me, I felt as if I had stopped. There I was ready to survive an Arctic winter and Julian Jenkins, one of the top UK Pros and a regular contributor to 220, went by in just Tri-shorts, a summer crop top and roll down sleeves. Awesome.

I put my head down and kept on going. Me, my Roo and my entire winter training wardrobe. Up the climb I went again, through the crowded areas by transition and out for my third lap. As I passed through the village I felt my back tyre go soft. I looked back and saw a flat. Fantastic. I changed it in about 8 minutes and was off again. But in a way it killed my fighting spirit. I went up the climb for the third time on the bike. The hill was getting harder and harder. Each time I was getting out of the saddle earlier on the rise. I could feel myself tiring. Finally I arrived in transition, changed my shoes, took off my helmet, and headed out for those last 8 miles on foot.

My legs were like jelly. This was becoming a familiar sensation. 8 miles to go, but I had nothing left in the tank. My cold had eventually caught up with me. I knew these 8 miles were going to take a long time. And they did. I don't even remember crossing the finish line. I'd definitely earned my sweatshirt on this one.

The Ballbuster lives up to its name. It is a great race. It's actually one of my favourite races of the UK calendar. Despite Julian Jenkins eclipsing me as he lapped me, I was pleased that he eventually went on to win. I think once he realised I had a cold and posed little threat that particular year, it was pretty plain sailing for him. In truth, it probably took the gloss off his victory knowing that although he'd beaten me, I wasn't at my best. I stayed on for the awards and a hot tea and cake in the National Trust shop. As I stood sipping my tea, I wondered whether they would spare an award for me. Cleanest bike? Most clothes worn? Quickest tyre change? Needless to say, I got in the car empty-handed, but knew it wouldn't be the last time I visited Box Hill and had my balls busted.

Chapter 19

Feet Like Blocks Of Ice

After the Ballbuster, the rest of November slipped by. December crept up, the days got shorter, the weather colder and I kept on with my little routine. After work I'd drive to the gym, go to a spinning class, go for a run, do some upper body weights and occasionally go for a swim. In fact, I was swimming so rarely I should have taken my goggles back to the shop. Swimming was still my least favourite and I couldn't get enthusiastic about it. Before a swim session I always had a sense of dread. However when I was actually in the pool, I really enjoyed it. Well, after the first 10 lengths anyway. On the other hand, I was staying on top of my cycling. I was really enjoying the spinning classes. I found spinning to be really motivational and with a run on the end, it was a good solid workout.

But in reality by the middle of December I was on standby, sitting with my engine idling. I was a gym bore rather than a true 'get out there whatever' triathlete. I was fit but I was tied to the gym. And what was most worrying was that I was eight months away from racing my first Ironman. It was here, in the middle of winter, that my commitment was challenged daily.

Whatever the weather I knew I needed to get out. So I pulled out my clothes. It was time to grin and bear it. I was learning fast that dressing for winter cycling is an art. An art that requires planning and patience and should never be rushed. Here was my meticulous routine. First put on the heart rate monitor strap. Be warned, there is nothing more galling than having put everything else on, only to look down and see the strap lying on the floor the wrong side of nine layers of clothing. The vest and the shirt would then go on. Next a short sleeved cycling top and shorts. Then another long sleeved top and my winter tights. Mind you, don't forget that pee before you pull the tights on. Oh yes, it's really awkward finding yourself once you've got so many layers on. I then put on socks, shoes and neoprene overshoes. I did these at this point because if I bent down with too many layers on top, I got dizzy with the heat and restricted circulation. Okay, I would be warm by now. What next? Long sleeved thin top, long sleeved cycle top, third long sleeved top. The forearms were pretty tight now. From here I'd go out to my bike and put the rest on out there. The rest consisted of maybe another sweatshirt, gloves, balaclava or hat, helmet and maybe a small pack raincoat. Could I move? Not really, but I relied on the fact that the requirement for great dexterity would be minimal during the ride. Getting dressed was a palaver and an art, often a stressful art. And like Murphy's Law, however many layers, however cold outside, however fast I tried, it always took me 15 minutes to get dressed. Can you imagine the result if after all of that I looked down to see the heart rate strap lying there? Let's just say it involved some tight jaw clenching and very blue language.

Finally, dressed like an Eskimo, I'd pull out the bike and I'd be ready to go. Well, not quite, as the inevitable was bound to happen. Yep, I'd need another pee. However much I tried to convince myself I'd be okay, pretend I could ignore it and it'd go away, it never did. Back into the house I would go and, with unveiled curses, I would twist, contort and wrestle with my clothes in order to find my manhood. Why would I pee for five minutes solid? I had relieved myself moments earlier, why didn't it come out then? One of the great universal questions of our time. It was little wonder why I struggled to ride, but then despite the initial drama of getting ready, winter riding itself was fun. I loved being out in the bleak conditions with wet roads, mulchy verges and bare hedges. Whichever direction I rode, there was a headwind. Once I was out, it was raw, vivid living.

Here I was, toughing it out. December was testing my resolve, out on my own, just me, every article of clothing I owned and my faithful Roo. It was without looking and through pure chance therefore that I made a new friend, a friend I now count on as one of my best friends. I was spinning mid-week and there was a guy in the spinning class, stocky, tanned, broad in the shoulder with a triathlon T-shirt on. Now I couldn't let the audacity of wearing a triathlon T-shirt to 'my' spinning class pass without a quiet word. So without further ado I confronted the upstart. 'Hello' I said, introducing myself and quizzing him on his T-shirt. His name was Simon. He'd done a couple of sprint races and he'd entered the UK Half-Ironman in Wales the following year. Well, who would have thought it, someone as abnormal as me. We got chatting. We lamented the difficulty of winter training, motivation and getting out and promptly arranged to keep each other company on a ride the following Saturday.

To say the weather got better in the days preceding the Saturday of our ride would be a blatant lie. But there was no stopping two would-be Ironmen. I called Simon on the Friday night to test his metal. Both as reluctant as each other to set out and face the elements, yet neither of us prepared to lose face, we arranged to meet the following morning. Pride, it's a powerful motivator. Saturday was bleak. I arrived 10 minutes before departure, pulled my bike out of the car boot and put on those extra layers. Simon arrived. Big smile and ready to go. Now this guy was either hard as nails or, despite the T-shirt and build, didn't get out much in the winter. Turns out it was a bit of both. A little uncertain of my ground and how he would react to my advice, I asked

'Do you have long leggings?'

He stood there defiantly in his shorts. I proffered some more advice without trying to appear a whimp.

'Do you want to borrow some gloves or a hat?'

I could see doubt creeping into his mind as he stood there in his shorts and two layers, toned but blue kneed, opposite me, dressed like an Eskimo who feels the cold. He took my spare hat and gloves, and on my advice pulled on his Ron Hill Tracksters, whilst confessing that he mainly went spinning in the winter. As a final act of goodwill, I ventured that he might want to put on a third top. He was wearing a short and long sleeved top, compared with my nine layers.

And we were off. We had a real laugh. As we rode north of Milton Keynes the wet ground turned into snow covered roads. We were probably out for about two hours and both really enjoyed it. Simon wore trainers with his toe clips and an hour into the ride I enquired whether his feet were cold. When we got back to the car he disappeared very quickly, telling me they hadn't been until I'd mentioned it.

Simon agreed to come to the gym's run group the following week. As we ran round he gingerly confessed he may have under-estimated the cold. We agreed to meet up again the following Saturday. I had created an instant bond with Simon, despite his audacity in 'my' spinning class to try and out trump me with a tri-shirt. I would learn he had drive, a great sense of humour and a real competitive streak. We ride most weekends these days. He's bought his own hat and gloves but still manages to survive with about half the layers I wrestle with. I'll never forget my first bike ride with him, snow on the ground, inadequately dressed, feet like blocks of ice, continually laughing and chatting away.

Chapter 20

Soaring With The Eagles

At last, December was over. I was now in the year of the Ironman. It wasn't as if there were birds in the trees, little lambs gambling around fields, bulbs poking their heads through the thawing frost, but winter was slowly, very slowly passing by. I knew I still had to spend time training in the gym and braving the elements at weekends, but I had survived the deepest, darkest, coldest weather winter could throw at me. Seven months to go and every day I was getting closer.

December had had its ups and downs. The ups? One, I had found a new training partner, Simon. Two, I had kept training consistently. Three, I had competed in The Great Barford Half-Marathon mid-December and run it in a respectable time of 1 hour and 33 minutes, The world record was still safe. The Downs? One, I fought a constant battle with self-doubt. Two, the weather. Three, motivation.

Finding a balance between over-training and being lazy was very difficult. It was hard to tell when I had overdone it and when I just needed a kick up the backside. As time moved on, finding this balance was possibly one of my biggest challenges. I was finding this a solitary game, self-motivation was critical and fatigue was pretty constant. If I was tired and didn't feel like training, I felt guilty. For all I loved training, sometimes sitting there in the car after work wondering which way to turn was hard. When my legs were heavy and I felt lethargic, should I train? Guilty if I didn't. More fatigue if I did.

What was my typical week?

Sunday – normally I did a 1 mile swim and some light upper weights with an hour long run or a 1 and a half to 2 hour bike ride. Monday – 1 mile swim and a 45 minute spinning class. Tuesday – 1 hour 30 minutes on the turbo trainer. I had bought a new quiet magnetic turbo trainer. Time still slowed significantly but I didn't have to turn the telly up so much. Wednesday – 1 mile swim and a 9 mile run. Thursday – upper body weights. Friday – rest day. Saturday – 2 hour bike ride.

This really was the life, but I felt tired and I had a little niggle in my hamstring. When to stop? When to rest?

When I look back my training made me fit but it was unstructured and had no progression. I train more consistently now and build up gradually. Plus I know far more about nutrition and replenishment. My training is more structured, with a plan developed by someone with proper sports qualifications. The results have been phenomenal. But back in 2001 I knew none of this.

One of the great pleasures for me in life is reading on the loo. Especially when we have people staying for the weekend. Quiet, quality time. I was flicking through the pages of 220 when the advert jumped out at me. 'Ironman Training Day' involving Matt Belfield, Ironman Lanzarote '98 runner up and '99 winner. Hello, this must be for me. I called the number straightaway. Well, I got off the loo first.

A little nervous, I spoke to a relaxed guy called Ian Mayhew, someone who was to become another friend with whom I would enjoy adventures and racing for years to come. After much reassurance from Ian that I wouldn't be out of my depth, I reserved my place and got very excited about meeting Matt Belfield and using his advice to launch my assault on a major Ironman crown.

The event took place on a Saturday in early January. I pulled into the car park in Hendon, North London, within the security perimeter fence of the training centre for the London Metropolitan Police. It was grey, overcast, wet and I was nervous. Here I was, with the pretension of being an Ironman, about to embark on an Ironman Training Day.

Ian had advised me to bring food, my bike, turbo trainer, swimming gear, trainers and warm clothes. I had packed my car as if I was going for the weekend. He had reassured me it would be a low-key day, offering advice to all levels. As ever, a deep-seated insecurity that I was a multisport fraud filled me with dread. I feared I would be hopelessly outclassed. On the phone I'd volunteered information, trying to find a way out. He'd assured me I'd be fine. I'd asked him if he'd ever raced an Ironman. Only six was the response. My nerves increased. I should have listened to the common sense voice in my head, but instead, with my devil may care attitude, I would no doubt humiliate myself. Full of reservations, I pulled out my over-full kit bag and started what would surely turn out to be the most embarrassing day of my life. My flaws would be exposed and I would fade humbly into a life of obscurity in my semi-detached in Milton Keynes, watching gardening and DIY shows.

I was greeted by Ian and his girlfriend. Both were very friendly and in no way intimidating. Ian was my build, slightly folically challenged, had a very dry sense of humour and a constant grin. I liked him instantly. As expected, there were a lot of folks there with big thighs in Ron Hill tracksters. The room was filled with the testosterone of a climbing hut without the beards. But as my eyes adjusted and furtively moved around the room, I caught the same nervous glances from others. As ever, my nerves subsided. Anticipation is always worse than reality. Most were as green as me. Nevertheless I was still terrified of the prospect of a group swim.

We all settled down and out came a guy called Nick. Nick, as I have discovered over the years, is the unluckiest person you'll ever meet. Disaster follows him everywhere. As a result he has the mick taken out of him constantly but he races valiantly and is always to be seen at the big races. He's a good guy and I have a lot of time for him. He was followed by a smaller guy, Matt Belfield, Ironman Lanzarote winner 1999. To me, that summed up his achievements. This guy had won a race that is rumoured to be the toughest on the planet. Shorter than I expected, tanned, stocky with a blond shock of curly hair, he had a warm smile, bright blue eyes and could quite easily make a few quid from modelling if all else failed.

He stood there smiling, probably more nervous than the knowledge hungry, Ron Hill clad no-hopers who sat in front of him. Nick introduced him and took us through the format. Over the course of the day we would do coaching sessions in the pool, on the turbo trainers and on the running track, all led by Matt. Between these sessions Matt would give us some pearls of wisdom, we would watch the Lanzarote 1999 race and there would be coaching tips thrown in for good measure. I settled back, ready to enjoy the day. Great, no pressure on me yet, just enjoy some stories.

'Right let's get started on the swim session,' Matt announced. My daydreams were shattered. Off to the pool. Humiliation was imminent.

There would be videoing of technique and feedback afterwards. My heart sank. Throw your washing in, as I flayed up the pool. Sorry Lisa. We changed, were seeded in lanes and did a quick warm up. I was slightly re-assured as I was actually placed in the middle lane. Okay, so I wasn't the fastest, but I wasn't the slowest. And for the next hour I followed the drill. I kept up and didn't shame myself. Maybe I had improved more than I gave myself credit for.

We changed, went back up to the main room and prepared for the video assessment onslaught. My turn got closer and closer. Eventually it arrived. 'Strong style'. From the winner of Lanzarote 1999. I almost fainted. If only Lisa has been here. It's funny how you dread things and they are never as bad as you think. Maybe I was more prepared for this Ironman than I thought. Okay, now the bit we'd all been waiting for. The life of an Ironman winner. So how did I need to adapt my routine?

Matt stood at the front and took us through his typical day. He was open, honest and not at all boastful. Just matter of fact. It was, quite simply, this was what I did to win, it hurt and it was hard work.

'Train 40 hours a week. Wake up at 6am, swim 4,000 metres. Eat, go back to bed. Wake, cycle for 5 hours. Go out for a 1 hour run. If you still feel good, get back on the turbo. 6 days a week.'

Was that all I had to do to win? My eyes watered. After a 4,000 metre swim at 6am, I'd struggle to get out of bed for the bike ride. If this was what it took to win an Ironman, the contenders at Lake Placid would be fairly safe from my challenge.

Matt had an amazing style. He knew beyond all others what abnormal behaviour was all about. He was quietly spoken, modest, there was no pretence, and there was no ego. He was telling his story and what he did. It sounded gruelling. Really gruelling. In fact, it became clear that he was a nutcase and quite simply lived in an extreme endurance world.

After winning Grotty (the 'in' abbreviation for Lanzarote) he qualified for Hawaii. To prepare for the conditions he did heat training on his turbo trainer in the shed. He would wear three pairs of leggings and seven sweatshirts and sit there pedalling away, often in the dark. Next to him he'd have a three gallon barrel of water. He'd go for 2 hours. I could hardly sit for 10 minutes on my turbo in just a pair of shorts without collapsing from heat exhaustion. He was nuts.

There he was in front of us and frankly, he was inspiring. For all of us in the room it was out of this world. He continued with many more revelations for his mesmerised audience.

It turned out that the 5 hour bike rides weren't as straightforward as you'd think. He'd average 20 to 22 miles per hour. Impressive. But he wouldn't use his racing bike. He wanted something slower to make the workout harder so that he'd feel a boost when racing on a lighter machine. But his training bike alone wasn't slow enough. So he fixed a pannier bag on and put two bricks in it. Hello, this was not normal.

Matt Belfield had become a bit of a legend in the cycling world the year he won Lanzarote. He would go along to 25 mile time trials, win them by a huge margin, but he would never be there for the awards. He'd head off to cycle some more. Asked how he fed on his training rides, the sports drinks manufactures will be devastated to hear his answer of

'Water mixed weakly with orange juice. Water on its own is boring.'

Up to this point, Matt Belfield was the toughest athlete I'd ever met. Before the build-up to his Lanzarote triumph he'd actually retired for a bit. Asked why he'd decided to come back into the sport he replied,

'However tough the training is, it beats the 9 to 5.'

Off to the turbo trainers. I was really enjoying this, re-assured that everyone was as awe-inspired as me. As I drizzled sweat over my bike, I was relieved that I was only wearing my running vest and cycling shorts. Seven sweatshirts and three pairs of leggings. I couldn't imagine it.

Back up the stairs for lunch and to watch the '99 race with live commentary from the winner. I had actually never seen an Ironman race, and here I was watching my first one with the guy who crossed the line first. I was excited for him. I couldn't imagine the emotions. There was footage of him on the beach before the swim start. So much pressure. He'd come second in 1998. Did he feel nervous?

'No. I was sure I'd done enough to win.'

And they were off. Surge, fury, confusion. The race had begun. His thoughts?

'Go as fast as you can for 2.4 miles. I saw who I was with and settled into a pace.'

It looked effortless. Just short of 50 minutes later, out of the water, up the beach, into transition. Matt grabbed his race bag, on to the bike.

'The bike felt good.'

He passed the leader early and started to build a lead. Lanzarote looked unforgiving. It was like the moon. Lunar, lava rock, deserts, vicious headwinds, burning sun, long climbs. Every pedal stroke was a fight. This was where he won the race. As the motorcycle cameraman filmed, his face was expressionless, fixed. His riding style, despite the conditions, looked effortless. He just drank, ate and pedalled relentlessly. He was there to win.

The bike was over. As he came into transition he unclipped his feet, wobbled his legs and got ready to start racing a marathon, to win his first Ironman. In the commentary, Matt was smiling, his eyes gleaming. I was excited for him just watching it. What must it have felt like to be there? Someone grabbed his bike, he pulled on his trainers, changed his sunglasses, pulled on a cap and he was off. He had built a lead of 15 minutes. The heat looked energy sapping and unforgiving.

'My guts were really hurting at this stage, too much grapefruit in my mix.' Apparently he used grapefruit to help absorb the carbohydrate.

As the video ran on, he stopped talking. He was watching with us, re-living that race, watching himself race a marathon on perhaps the greatest day of his life. He won. He smiled. What a moment. There we sat facing an Ironman champion.

He sat back in his chair. He was king of the world, impassable, untouchable, soaring. He'd gone on to Hawaii, a favourite to win following his victory in Lanzarote. But despite the shed preparation, he'd cramped with the heat early in the bike and fallen away as a contender. Would he ever get back? His routine was rigorous but he'd been plagued with injuries since and hadn't yet regained form. He was modest, friendly, open and driven. I thought he was an amazing guy. I hoped he'd rediscover his form. I hoped he'd sit again, smiling, watching another victory.

Onto the third workout of the day, out on the track. For the final session the format was simple, we had to run at a specific low-intensity heart rate around a running track. The purpose of the workout was to demonstrate the value of training at a low intensity to improve base stamina, make energy consumption more efficient and enable recovery from higher intensity sessions. As we looped around the track running at our own specific heart rates, it was the strongest possible test of my will power as others passed me. I knew I couldn't react and maintain my heart rate. I guess deep down I am quite competitive. The session highlighted to me that not all training needs to be balls to the wall to achieve improvement. Low-intensity training was a fad I felt I could certainly see myself subscribing to. We did the session and the day ended. We all thanked Matt, wished him luck and thanked Ian. It had been a really useful and reassuring day. I was better prepared than I thought. I was re-inspired. I had 200 days to go, 28 weekends. It was time to get serious.

Chapter 21

Life With gearsandtears.com

The next six weeks flew by. Suddenly it was early March. After the Ironman Training Day at Hendon, I had put my head down and got serious about training. Ian Mayhew and his crew seemed like a good bunch and they had more events coming up so, as I wasn't affiliated to any club, I joined theirs, gearsandtears.com, which was run by Ian. As I renewed my BTA licence I proudly completed the club box. I also paid the extra £5 for International Endorsement, therefore being insured to race overseas. For an extra fiver I was now an International Athlete, well, at least on paper.

Winter was gradually relenting. The days were getting longer and milder, the layers of clothing less. I had reflected on Hendon and Matt Belfield. His efforts were superhuman and his results spoke for themselves. I would never train full time, firstly because of work but, more critically, I really didn't believe my body and health would survive. Not to mention my marriage. But as I drove home from Hendon, I had decided it was time to up the ante.

First off, I would train like I'd never trained before. And secondly, I would eat like I'd never eaten before.

It was time to up everything. Where I would normally swim 60 lengths in the pool I'd do 100. It was time to lose my fears about swimming with others. It was time to stop skulking in the shadows, afraid of an embarrassing effort. Straight after the Training Day I had gone down to Milton Keynes Triathlon Club and joined their coached swim sessions. On the first night I was seeded in the second slowest lane but after six weeks of not missing a session my swimming had improved tenfold. I also realised that I needed to get both bike and running miles into my legs. Turbo training was okay in the week but it was time to get dressed up and stay out at the weekends. I upped my average weekend bike ride from a mere 1 hour and 30 minutes to a minimum of 3 hours. Up until Hendon, I'd been obsessed with how many miles I'd covered. Now I was doing timed sessions. Over the coming months I would build up to rides in excess of 5 hours. I had attacked the last six weeks and really put in a good effort. In retrospect, I'd probably upped the ante too quickly. I was tired but I'd survived.

My progress with running wasn't as good as I'd have liked. I'd strained the outside of my right knee, my ITB, doing some quad extensions and had struggled for five weeks with no real progress on the healing front. I'd been to an osteopath but made little progress. Gung ho to the bitter end, I threw caution aside and decided to just get out and run. Foolhardy? Sometimes you just get lucky as, quite extraordinarily, my folly paid off and my knee got better. Years on, and with far more experience, I don't recommend this to anyone. Now I am a firm believer in stretching and spend a good 15 minutes stretching before I get into bed every night. But this time my folly didn't punish me. I was back on my pins and winter was almost behind me.

I had followed some great advice from Matt as well. Get off road with the runs. I went along canals, up to the woods, ran on bridle paths. I had to be constantly vigilant, watching the feet, watching the ankles and not taking my eyes off the ground. The odd protruding root could be murderous. But it was heaven on the knees.

In truth, Hendon had made me realise I had to stop pussyfooting around and underestimating my own ability. I realised I had developed a 'I never get picked in the playground because I'm rubbish at football' mentality and therefore persuaded myself that I was rubbish. My own lack of confidence had stopped me joining a structured swim session for fear of humiliation, or a competitive running club for the same reason. Hendon had actually proved to me that I had developed a good level of fitness and could comfortably hold my own with fit folks. I had to get in and mix it. Up until now I'd run with a good bunch of guys from the gym, but was not really being pushed. Without further ado, after six months of procrastinating, I went down to Milton Keynes Athletics Club and joined their Tuesday and Thursday night sessions. There were probably between 40 and 60 runners each time and I instantly enjoyed these sessions. There was a very high standard of running but each time I found myself finishing in the top ten percent. As we followed the footpath for miles around Milton Keynes on the various tough sessions, it was like a human train, charging down any haphazard pedestrian who happened to get in the way. I cursed myself for having let my self-doubt hold me back.

Life was great, if not without its mistakes and lessons. The first time I upped my time out on the bike, I ran out of energy at just over 2 hours. First lesson in nutrition. I wasn't Matt, able to survive for hours on weak orange squash. Next time out, I loaded on the carbohydrate bottles. Orange squash may make water less boring but PSP22 gives it a real kick. Also, my tender bits got a lot more tender, in fact on the long rides they were disconcertingly numb. Time for a new saddle. If I was losing the feeling from the lower part of my body over 3 hours, what would 6 hours be like? It didn't bear thinking about. I went out and bought a new saddle with a cut out down the middle to relieve the pressure on the main nerve stem which runs through the groin and enjoyed an instant improvement.

Then there was the back of my neck, my shoulders and my back. They really hurt with the extra time out. I could hardly stand up at the end of the ride, never mind run. Linds would massage them and it would ease but I had to do something here. I hoped over time they would stretch out but I feared it could well be my old spinal injury. I raised the handlebars once again, getting a steeper angled stem. It all helped. Something I was learning was that every time I encountered a problem, I was working out a way to fix it. The Ironman was an inevitability. If something stood in the way, I just had to figure a way through.

Time was moving on. With it being almost March, the new season was nearly on me. While I sat on the loo I would religiously pour over the event listings, working out my race plan for the 2001 season. I was looking at a Sprint Triathlon in Stratford-upon-Avon in early May. Then next up would be Milton Keynes Olympic Triathlon in late May. Then on to Bournemouth Olympic Triathlon in early June, followed by the old favourite river swim in the Windsor Olympic Triathlon in mid June. That, I reasoned, would see me race fit. Then in the run up to Lake Placid I'd planned to up my distance on the Weymouth Half-Ironman which took place five weeks before Ironman Lake Placid. Then to finish off the season I'd perhaps join Simon in the Half-Ironman in Wales in

September. Ambitious? Maybe. Time would tell. Added to the above I also had some club events. Both Milton Keynes Triathlon Club and gearsandtears.com ran a series of duathlons during the spring and summer. But it was gearsandtears.com which provided the true adventure, with events such as the Surrey Slog, Chainbreaker, Monsterman and Hollybourne Hellraiser. You get the theme? And these events certainly lived up to their names.

The inaugural event was the Surrey Slog, a challenging cross-country duathlon (run, bike, run). Excited at the first race with my new club, I left home early to get down to the start, high in the windswept North Downs. It was in the middle of nowhere, in a muddy car park on the ridge of the Downs. There was a huge field of 10 foolhardy racers who set off on a staggered time trial format start across the challenging cross-country run. Covered in mud, we then had to leap onto our bikes and charge around the bike course. By the start of the second run I was completely knackered but delighted to find myself in second place. I was determined to prove I was worthy of racing for gearsandtears.com. I held my position and finished in second place. Okay, hardly a resounding positioning on a national scale but I'd raced hard. It was a great race and, in the spirit of all the gearsandtears.com events, a non-conventional format added some interest to what is actually not a very varied UK calendar. The gearsandtears.com strapline is 'Not for the faint hearted'. Have a go at a race and you'll see why. I should also mention the flapjack and tea served by Ian's Mum and Dad throughout, which are exceptional and do wonders for a chilled soul.

I was determined to get as much experience as possible. Ian had also organised a road bike Track Day at Eastway cycle track in north London, so I booked myself a place. Buoyed by my new self confidence, I also entered a series of national duathlon events run by Milton Keynes Triathlon Club at the Milton Keynes Bowl. I, too, probably wouldn't stick around for the awards, but was sure my absence wouldn't be felt as keenly as Matt Belfield's.

The last six weeks had been fantastic. Highs, lows and elation. My whole being was still focused on one day. It was all consuming and thrilling.

Chapter 22

Not Sensible Behaviour

Not behaving normally was fine. Not behaving sensibly, on the other hand, had finally caught up with me. I had pushed myself too hard and my body had given way. The cold had started very subtly on the weekend of the Surrey Slog. It had been an early start and I'd pushed myself hard during the race. Afterwards I'd taken my Grandma out for lunch and then gone to a party in the evening. And what a great party. It was themed Stars in Your Eyes. Linds was surprised that I refused her suggestion to join forces with Neil and Jackie and go as Abba. Neil and I had other plans. Neil arrived dressed as Alice Cooper's twin. And as for me, 'Well, tonight Matthew, I'm going to be Marilyn Manson.' With long-haired wigs and make-up we both got into character. I had way too many tequilas. I always know I've had too much to drink when I close my eyes in the shower and almost fall over.

On the Sunday I got up with the hangover from hell but, clinging to my resolve, went out for my 3 hour bike ride in the pouring rain. My cold grew a little worse but, unperturbed and with no regard for what might be a sensible course of action, I continued on the Monday with my 100 lengths in the pool and 45 minutes of spinning. On Tuesday I felt as if someone had sandpapered my throat. But it would take more than a sore throat to stop me, so I merrily kept on training and that night went to run with Milton Keynes Athletics Club. It was a cold and damp evening, in the region of minus one to minus two degrees and, predictably enough, the cough moved from my throat to my chest. I can see the medics of the world wincing. But I was always looking for the positive and concluded that at least all the coughing was doing my abs the power of good. Now, in my defence, by the weekend I realised I was ill and though I had entered a half-marathon, I decided it would be a good idea to pull out. But then the Saturday was a long day to do nothing. So after a morning of twiddling my thumbs, by the middle of the afternoon I was dressed up and out on the Roo, toughing it out for 2 hours in a 25mph headwind. I went for a second ride on the Sunday. Well, come on, I didn't do the half-marathon. Were these the telltale signs of someone losing it?

By Sunday evening my cough was coming on nicely. My hacking made the Marlboro Man look like Jane Fonda. I was falling apart. Finally, to add insult to injury, or injury to illness, we had gone indoor skiing (I know, I am ashamed of myself and deserve everything I got) and tweaked my knee and shin on a bad landing off a jump. I was showing off at the time.

By not recognising when to take my foot off the pedal and rest, I had run myself into the ground. In a state of health where most would have taken a few days off work, here I was training like an idiot. I was sleeping badly, I was constantly coughing and my body just came to a halt. On the following Monday I had climbed into the car, intent on getting to the pool, and there I had sat. As I contemplated which way to turn, two tracks played on the stereo. I started the car, reversed out of the space and pointed the front wheels towards home. Three slices of cheese on toast with tomato ketchup later and I felt glum. Guilty. Why? I was ill to the point where I wasn't sleeping. But still I felt guilty.

I can't make this point enough. Ironman, it's an obsession. It is with you all the time, over you, in you, consuming you. The funniest thing was, as I sat there feeling glum, I realised you can do a hell of a lot in the evening when you're not training. Up until then I had lived in my own little world. I left work between 5.30pm and 6pm, trained, got home about 8.30pm, spent time with Linds, cooked, ate, washed up, slept.

Now I was home at 6pm and the evening was long. What do normal people do? On principle, I decided I couldn't turn the TV on. Well, actually, there was no principle involved at all. I had turned it on and everything showing was rubbish. So I'd turned it off. Who would watch EastEnders? I would rather pull my toenails off with pliers. So what to do? I had read my book, cooked a meal. Where was Linds? Still at work. She really did work too hard. I had already called her about four times encouraging her to come home. I read some more. Wow, the evening was long but, strangely, I felt better. The following night we'd planned to go out for a meal. Two nights in a row of not training. My Ironman training regime was falling apart. I'd booked the table weeks before for 8.30pm in anticipation of a quick swim before the starter. So there I was, 6pm all alone, holding a lonely vigil until 8.00pm. Linds was so used to me not being there until later that she had developed her own work patterns and evening activities around it. She had called to say she would be home shortly. Even shortly takes a long time sometimes. I read a bit more, tidied the house up, put the vac round, read some more. Time, when you're home and alone, moves at another speed. Linds got home, we went out and time sped up.

It was strange. I had worn myself out, *really, really* out. It was sensible to stop and I should have stopped and rested much earlier. But I felt so guilty for not training. Not training had made me realise how important and valuable it was to me. Until now, I'd thought it was just a hobby. But really it was a passion. It ran through me, inspired me, made me. I couldn't live a life of getting home at 6pm and going through to 10pm without doing something. I had to be fulfilled. Maybe I'd always thought training was a bit pointless. I was a hamster on a wheel. But now I'd realised the cage was pretty unfulfilling without the wheel. For the first time ever, I really looked forward to swimming the following night.

The end of March crept up, the days were getting considerably warmer and my cold was long gone. Inspired by Matt Belfield, I had two and a half months of solid training behind me and felt fitter than I had ever felt before. I felt I was in the zone, really in balance. What was more, I was really enjoying it. I wanted to do more. My typical training week now consisted of:

Monday – 30 to 45 minute swim, usually drills or intervals (alternating between high intensity and recovery periods). I was trying to teach myself to breath bilaterally, i.e. on both sides, however my efforts on the left hand side typically resulted in half the pool passing into my stomach. I would then get out, quickly dry off and go on to do a 45 minute spinning class.

Tuesday – run club with Milton Keynes Athletics Club. This typically consisted of a 1 hour to 1 hour 20 minute run made up of gruelling intervals.

Wednesday – I would swim between 30 and 60 minutes and head

out smelling of chlorine, with fresh goggle rings branded across my eyes, for another 45 minute spinning class.

Thursday – swim with Milton Keynes Triathlon Club. 1 hour of intervals. Despite my fears I kept up well. If I was feeling brave I would do a 45 minute to 1 hour run before the swim. But this usually resulted in my dying halfway through the swim, as my energy levels hit rock bottom and the power faded.

Friday – night off.

Saturday – typically a minimum 3 hour bike ride.

Sunday – a 1 hour 45 minute to 2 hour bike ride.

On balance, I probably should have been swimming a little less and running a little more. But the swim really was the one I feared.

Amazingly I still got time to see Linds and my employer hadn't sacked me yet. Quite clearly I was obsessed. I tried to balance the sessions so they weren't all full on. I reasoned I should balance hard, short sessions with less intense but longer endurance sessions and technique work focusing on control. With summer approaching the weather began to improve, making it easier to get out at the weekends. I was still dressed like a cold-sensitive Eskimo, but it was reassuring that on some rides the clothes felt stuffy and restrictive. I knew it would soon be April and then we would be into those long, heady summer nights.

I was loving the cycling. On the road I nearly always took out of Milton Keynes there was a sign two miles from my house that read 'City Limit'. As I rolled past it I would smile and feel the thrill of freedom, knowing I had three hours to fill just getting lost in the countryside. I would head out in one direction and then just take random turns, exploring somewhere new. Invariably I would come to a junction I recognised and would then head off in another direction. The clock would tick down and I would just ride at a nice steady pace. The miles would fall away. I always seemed to have a headwind, my feet would be cold, my shoulders would get tight, sweat would drip and dry on the inside of my glasses. I would ride past newly ploughed fields, knarled trees, ponds, old cottages, up long hills, down steep roads and through chicanes, past pubs and people out walking, all wrapped up. All would be gone in a second. I'd be in and out of the saddle, on bumpy roads, rattling along, swerving to avoid potholes. And sometimes, very rarely, the road would be perfectly smooth, the wind would push from behind and the Roo would glide, surging underneath me. Riding was exhilarating.

I would even fall off. The sign of a true cyclist. One time going into a junction, the back wheel slipped out on a bad camber. There was a scrape of pedal, a dull knock on my knee, hip, elbow and there I was down on one side, sliding along, sweeping up the gravel. I was wearing so many clothes that I just bounced, unhurt, if not a little shaken. The greatest damage was to my pride.

Time was at last flying by. We had been skiing the previous month and enjoyed a great week in France. All the time I prayed that I wouldn't hurt myself. It seemed as though I blinked and that holiday was already four weeks behind us and it was now the end of March. Only four months to go.

PART 3

Walking The Tightrope

Chapter 23

The Final Touches

I was trying hard to convince myself that winter had gone. The racing season was now imminent. It was time to put the finishing touches to my pre-season preparation. Having spent months endlessly turning at each end of the pool, enduring rain, wind, hail and snow on my bike and pounding the redways of Milton Keynes dressed in arctic exploration gear, it was time to see how fit I really was. gearsandtears.com had organised another training day, this time at the Eastway cycle track in North-east London. Hungry for more top tips, I jumped in the car and headed down.

Eastway cycle track is an outdoor circuit where the great Eddie Meryks rode some legendary races. It is just over a mile long, across an undulating, fast, technical course where you're either on the gas clattering up the gears or dabbing the brakes and dropping your shoulder through a bend. The training day was certainly not for the faint-hearted. Eastway is also in a very rough part of London. As I parked my car next to a burned out van, I hoped I'd see it again. This was bandit country. After a warm welcome from Ian, we got down to business. We would have a 45 minute ride on the track for a warm up, applying some of the coaching tips we'd been given, and then go into an hour long Madisson, a multi-lap points format sprint race. My heart leapt into my mouth. The demons were whispering.

In the clubhouse before we started, all the newcomers gave a short overview of their racing CVs. A lean American woman, probably in her mid forties, listed off all her racing triumphs and as she rolled off her achievements, I felt smaller and smaller. She mentioned about 10 Ironman finishes, completing Hawaii three times, the Marathon Des Sables, multiple Comrades Marathons and an Eco Challenge to boot. In short, a CV I was in awe of. I chuckled as Ian called from the back,

'Yeah, but have you done any long stuff?'

I didn't think it would be worth mentioning that I had racked up two Spelthorne Sprint Triathlon finishes. Yeah, that's right, not just the one, I went back for a second time. I kept very quiet. It felt as though there were 20 others in the room with equally impressive CVs. As ever, I felt way out of my league and about to face certain abject humiliation. And to top it all, there was the uncertainty about whether I would ever see my car again.

Now the racing format for this Madisson was a rolling three laps before the start, then the bell would sound and we'd race for an hour. Once we'd started, every time the bell rang on a lap, the top five finishers of that lap would accumulate points. Basically it would be an hour long sprint race. My heart sank.

The race rolled off. On the first lap there was a warm banter in the bunch. On the second lap, things were a bit quieter. On the third, the pace picked up significantly. But my nerves had settled. This was amazing. Here I was in a bunch in a bike race, living my childhood dreams. As we flew up towards the start, I wasn't sure quite what I was doing leading the front group.

I heard the bell and we were off. Furious pedalling, acceleration, down to the hairpin, round and out of the saddle, keep on the lead bike's rear wheel. Up over the rise. Keep working, stay in contention. Don't miss out on the points. What was I doing? I held the wheel, head down, I had seen this in the Tour de France. Stay out of the wind and keep my legs fresh. We flew down the straight. There were three of us. Me, a guy called Kiersey, and another called Dave. Where was Miss Endurance? Where were the demons? Hang on, where was Ian Mayhew? Up over the rise, down through the sweeping left and up to the finish. I took the podium points. Me, double Spelthorne finisher? The bell rang again. Oh no, another fast lap. Kiersey said something to me about going for it and contesting the sprints. 'Okay' I said, and then he just pulled away. He was off on his own. I dropped back with Dave who had joined another group and raced a tactical race, keeping out of the wind and taking points where I could. Overall I came second. Maybe I'd had a much better Spring than I thought. I was learning to ignore the demons and self-doubt. I had transformed myself over the winter from a novice triathlete to a respectable endurance athlete. What was more, my car was still in one piece.

It had been another great day with gearsandtears.com. As I pulled out of the car park I felt much more confident about my chances. I had proved to myself that I could at least mix it with experienced Ironmen. The question I had to answer was how would I fair over distance? There was only one way to find out, cycle 112 miles and drop a run on to the end. But before that little test, with a good day's racing under my belt, I headed into central London to meet with Dave and see another heavy metal gig. By the end I was dead on my feet and glad to get home.

The next week flew by and with Linds away the following Saturday I decided it was time for a test. It was time to see what 112 miles felt like with just me, the Roo, some food and drink. I left the gym car park at 9.30am with the intention of being back for 12.30pm to meet Simon so he could accompany me on the second half of the ride. Then with the ride complete, I would run for an hour and 30 minutes, just to see what that felt like. I probably did need therapy at this stage. But it seemed a good plan.

The first half of the ride disappeared quite easily. With the wind, the odd rain shower and a bit of sun, I was back at the gym for 12.30 and refuelled. It turned out that Simon couldn't make it after all so I set off on the second half alone. As the day wore on the wind filled in. Nature was doing everything possible to grind me to a standstill. I estimated I had enjoyed a blustery 20 mph headwind from mile 30 to mile 90. They were hard, grinding miles. With the wind pushing me back, at some points on the flat I was barely doing 10 miles per hour. It was soul destroying. As I passed gateways and gaps in the hedges, the strength of the side wind would try and whisk the bike away from under me. It was blowing. I felt every pedal stroke, worked for every metre, and then at mile 90, I turned for home and flew like an arrow. The Roo had never gone so fast over such a distance. It roared forward. As I crossed Milton Keynes on the smooth tarmac I was flying at a consistent 28 mph on the flat. Heaven.

In total, I had covered 113.25 miles. The 0.25 mile seemed extremely important at that point. With probably the slowest transition in history, I prepared myself for the run. I very carefully put my bike in the boot of the car and meandered rather than walked to the gym to change into dry gear. Sitting on the bench in the changing room, sipping energy drink, I slowly fastened my trainers. To turn out from the gym and do an hour and a half of running felt heartbreaking. My body was running close to empty. The voice of reason argued 'You've had a good day, time to head home.' I stood, picked up my bottle of energy and shuffled out. An hour and a half to go.

After 10 minutes the ache in my legs eased off and my shuffle turned into a jog, although admittedly it never materialised into a run. I'm not really sure where I went. Time disappeared. I actually ran for an hour and 40 minutes. It was really great to get back and sit down at the gym. I had amazed myself. In total I'd been out for nine hours. I was exhausted, hungry and very happy. My face was taut and red from the wind and the sun. The salt was dry and in my eyes. As I stretched in the gym, I couldn't quite believe I had been on the go for nine hours. What a day. Epic. I knew I still had more in the tank. It boosted my confidence no end. I was really starting to feel ready for the Ironman.

But to my surprise that Saturday really took its toll and I needed much longer to recover than expected. When I got home, I ate and ate and ate. Surprisingly for me, I took Sunday off. I felt very tired. However, with renewed vigour on Monday, it was time to get back into the swing of things. A quick 30 minutes in the pool and then on to Ricky's spinning class. Now my legs didn't feel quite right. During the fast sections, Ricky would be urging us to sprint. I'd tell my legs to sprint but they had other plans. This lack of power was even more marked on the Tuesday. At the Milton Keynes Athletics Club, on the interval sessions I would normally be in the top three or four within each interval. To my horror, I barely clung to the back of the group. I was really struggling. Saturday had obviously stripped all my reserves. As ever, just like with my cold, it took too long for me to see the writing on the wall. Rather than recognise that continuing to train was futile and I would be better off resting, I pushed on with gritted teeth and sheer determination. That was until I finally hit the wall. On Saturday I went for the shortest bike ride I have ever been on. I set out, and five minutes later I was opening the garage door and putting the Roo away. I was just tired, uninspired and not ready for a ride. I felt nothing. All week my mind had been telling my body to go. Finally the mind had given up. With hindsight, I recognise this as a classic case of over-training. I needed some rest. I took the next three days off, eating ridiculous amounts of food and doing absolutely nothing. By day four I felt plump. The tanks had been at least partially replenished and I'd learned another really useful lesson. It's not just about training hard. It's about recharging, recovering and being sensible. Well, most of the time.

My long ride had probably been too long. Doing 80 to 90 miles with maybe a 30 minute run would have done just the same, but hindsight is a beautiful thing. It also made clear to me how important fuelling and nutrition would be over distance. I had drunk a lot on the bike ride over the seven hours, eight 750 ml bottles of energy drink. I'd also eaten a Tracker bar or banana every 50 to 60 minutes, but had found my appetite for solids went around the 70 mile mark. I would really have to watch this at Lake Placid. On the run, I'd used another 750ml bottle of energy drink. Obviously this level of consumption was borderline in terms of being enough. It had got me round but had also dug deep into my energy stores. I had to plan carefully here. The bike ride at Lake Placid would follow a 2.4 mile swim which would undoubtedly take its toll. I needed to think this through carefully. It had been a very useful weekend.

There was also a final lesson from the weekend. Don't read the bike course profile in bed before turning the light off. There I was fast sleep when, in my dreams, my faithful demons whisked me to the start of Ironman Lake Placid. As the start gun got ever closer, I just couldn't find my goggles. My heart was racing. The demons skipped me forward to the bike transition. Where were my shoes? Stop messing with me.

Chapter 24

The Fast And The Furious

Finally it happened. Summer was on its way. Simon, Neil and I celebrated by meeting after work and riding for 20 miles without the need for lights. Joy, joy, joy. There was no better feeling in the world. Months of turbo training and spinning were behind us. Mind you, hold no illusions about the temperature. It was very cold. Even in May we were getting the odd snow flurry. Greenhouse effect my arse. But what a watershed, mid-week bike rides. Despite the cold, we knew a great summer would unfold ahead. I was invigorated. Suddenly things were happening. We had planned our first 10 mile team time trial in a week's time and the Stratford Sprint Triathlon was the following weekend.

Eventually I recovered from my 'Big Saturday' and my training got back into a routine. Everything seemed to be back in balance. My swimming was strong and I had clocked my first sub 25 minute mile. A huge milestone in my mind. Maybe swimming wasn't so bad after all. With the Eastway experience, Big Saturday and swimming like a fish, I was chomping at the bit.

With the local 10 mile time trial event to start the season off, it was time to get fast and furious. For some reason I got unnecessarily worked up over it. I think it was due to the fact that cycling has always been my passion. From an early age I have dreamed of racing my bike. After watching the Tour de France in my teens I had always dreamed of life as a Pro, grinding up mountains, winning summit finishes and splitting the field with daring breaks. But time trialling, in my mind, was something else altogether. It was the stuff of legends. All my heroes had been great time trialists, Lemond, Indurain, and recently Armstrong. To me, this discipline was the ultimate test. Balls to the wall, you and your bike against the clock and the field.

Okay, so maybe I was a little worked up about a rather low key, local club 10 mile event, out on the country lanes surrounding Milton Keynes. But I just didn't see it like that. For me this was the stadium of dreams, the moment of truth my 15 years of riding had been about. I even had a little wind down (a taper) during the week leading up to it, dropping the length of my ride on Sunday to keep my legs fresh. Sad, I know.

I had persuaded Neil and Simon it would be a good idea for us to race together. We were all racing the Stratford Triathlon and I convinced them it would put a little speed in their legs. We rolled up on the Monday night 30 minutes before the start, all a little bug eyed and in awe of the prospect of the race of truth. While we prepped our bikes in the car park, Neil, who had forgiven me long ago for the Spelthorne Sprint Triathlon the previous September, was once again giving me the 'you've stitched me up, Staples' glances.

We warmed up and got to the start for the allocated time. As we rode in formation, taking turns at the front and trying to get the rolling formation right, nerves were on edge and the tension was building. We lined up in our starting formation and suddenly we were off.

The race was actually a bit of a damp squib. Very quickly we learned that team time trialling, contrary to popular belief, wasn't about balls to the wall effort, but instead how well you ride as a unit. We were a shambles and our formation from start to finish was in complete disarray, one of us continually pulled off the front or fell off the back. We were stop start throughout the race and never really found our rhythm. Consequently, as soon as it had started, it was over. It was great fun but these Three Amigos had hardly set the world of time trialling on fire with our efforts.

Next up was the Stratford Sprint Triathlon. At last, real racing in anger. After the long winter I felt like a caged animal ready to be released. We had endured six months of cold winter training. I was raring to go.

As the weekend of Stratford got closer, the weather deteriorated. Saturday arrived and we were faced with a cold stiff north-westerly wind, blowing 25 mph. Despite being 'only' a Sprint this was not going to be without its challenges. The previous weekend I had been riding with five layers, leggings, overshoes, gloves and even a hat under my helmet. The prospect of leaping out of a pool, drenched in my racesuit and jumping on the bike in a stiff cold wind hardly inspired me. Still you pay your money and you take your chances. We climbed into the car and headed for the great playwright's hometown.

Without a doubt the Stratford Sprint Triathlon is a great race, in fact I would go as far as to say it's a showcase race. The format is staggered individual starts in a 25 metre pool, rather than a mass start. You swim 500 metres and then go out onto the bike for 12 miles. The bike course is simply three sides of a triangular route in the Warwickshire countryside, with only one real hill. Then comes a 3 mile run course. This year the route had been altered as the UK was being ravaged by foot and mouth disease. Therefore we would zig and zag around a field or two for 3 miles. Stratford is a massive race in the UK calendar, with a huge field of competitors. It is held in the local sports centre and also has a big Triathlon Expo. I thoroughly recommend it as both a novice and experienced racer event. The racing goes on all day, due to the staggered starts. Neil was scheduled to set off first, then Simon and I would follow on about 30 minutes later.

We went to cheer Neil off. He had a good swim and was quickly in transition. Again, as he pulled on his cycling shoes in transition he was cursing me and casting me dagger looks. As if it was my fault. Simon set off too, braving it in his Speedos. With the Half-Ironman coming up at the end of the summer Simon had to play it cool, acting the experienced veteran as he came through transition. I cheered him on, making a mental note to take the piss about the skimpy Speedos, and then it was my turn.

Time to get ready. As ever, final toilet. Down to the start and I was off. As I surged up the first 25 metres, my 2001 triathlon season had officially started. I was determined this was going to be a quick and earnest race. My swim was strong, up and down the pool, taking 8 minutes and 25 seconds to cover 500 metres (108th overall). I had planned my transition down to the smallest detail, no messing around today with towel and socks. I sprinted from the pool out into transition. I'd carefully counted the racks to my bike, critical in such a big transition area. There's always a number of unfortunate fools running around like headless chickens losing time because they can't find their racking point. I pulled on my shoes, helmet and glasses, clipped my number belt around my waist, grabbed my bike and sprinted to the mounting area.

I joined the traffic, clipped my feet in and put my head down. It was time to race. My fears of being too cold in the biting wind evaporated as I hunched over my aerobars and turned the pedals as quickly as I could. I flew down the first side of the triangle, the wind pressing on my back and bum. I turned the corner onto the bottom leg of the triangle and the wind hit my face. I just kept pedalling. Everyone was facing the same conditions, just go as hard as possible. I focused on the bike ahead and tried to catch it. Onto the last side of the triangle, up the long hill. 'Just stay low on the aerobars and keep trying to overtake', I coached myself. Over the top and then the long descent into town. I was pleased with the bike ride. Just over 40 minutes with an average speed of 21.6 mph (my split was 66th fastest). Suddenly I was back in transition. I dismounted and ran to my racking point, (again count the racks back in or you'll never find those trainers). Bike racked, helmet off, glasses off, bike shoes off, trainers on. Now despite my planning, I lost valuable seconds here. I still hadn't bought any quick fastening cleats for my laces and my hands and fingers were numb and stiffened from the cold. I fumbled tying my laces, set off, and they came undone three minutes later. I hastily tied them again with warmer fingers and set about the business of overtaking people.

The run zigged and zagged over a complicated course covering about two and a bit fields. I just kept trying to reel in the runner ahead of me. I had a few tussles with some quick runners, always watching my feet and ankles on the uneven route and suddenly there was the finish. I was very chuffed with the run, 18 minutes 55 seconds for 3 miles (my split was 21st fastest on the run). Neil, Simon and I had all raced well. Neil seemed less keen to kill me once he had finished and was all smiles again. How fickle.

We stopped for a beer, congratulating ourselves on picking such a great sport. I slept well that night. Despite the incident with the laces, (lace cleats were bought from the Expo after the race), the day had gone to plan. Overall I had come 48th out of some 550 racers. I was no longer feeling the fraud, the outsider, a gym bore pretending to be a triathlete. I was no longer the novice, merely surviving events. I had raced with purpose, planned well and made conscious decisions based on experience. Okay, so it was 'only' a Sprint, but I felt I had made huge progress since last season.

Summer was here and the racing just continued. The Three Amigos were back in the Stadium of Dreams the following Tuesday for the Milton Keynes Triathlon Club Duathlon. To their credit, Milton Keynes Triathlon Club have a healthy race calendar with some very competitive athletes. The personality behind the club is a guy called Mark Booth. Mark is very personable, always friendly, with a phenomenal racing CV. With Mark at the helm, they organise some very professional races and the Duathlon Series they run at The Bowl is no exception to this. On a closed circuit, the races are tough and fast contests. That Tuesday's race was a 3 mile run around the perimeter of Furzton Lake, back to transition, a 12 mile multi-lap bike circuit on a closed loop of the Bowl's service road, into transition and another 3 mile loop around Furzton Lake. You could enter as an individual or as part of a relay team.

To cut a long story short, I finished fourth in the race. But my transition lost me time. I was a little gutted with my cycling shoes. I had come in first from the run out of the individual competitors, but three people passed me in transition as I fumbled and fussed with the straps of my mountain bike shoes. I was still in fourth position in the individual field by the second transition, but again lost valuable seconds to the guy in third place by fiddling with my bike shoes. Luckily I had my toggle fastening laces and was soon in hot pursuit. However, whinge as I might, I was never going to catch Trevor, who was comfortably in third place. I ran with Trevor at Milton Keynes Athletics Club, I knew the speed he could generate and therefore knew he was gone. I gritted my teeth and held on to fourth place. Again I was delighted. My smile ran from ear to ear.

With three races behind me I concluded that Matt Belfield's advice had put me in good stead for the season ahead. I was a little worried about my transition, but clung to the wise words of Ian Mayhew, six times Ironman veteran,

'The longer the race, the slower the transition.'

What would a few seconds be over 12 to 14 hours? I was two and a half months away from Ironman Lake Placid. I was racing well and felt like Superman.

Chapter 25

First Out Of The Water

I was still giddy and flushed by my newly acquired super-powers when May fell away and I was in the season proper. June had brought the warm weather and I continued on, buoyed by my recent triumphs. However, I was about to come crashing down.

After the intoxication of the Stratford Triathlon and the Milton Keynes Duathlon I was really excited about the season. Next up was the Milton Keynes Olympic Triathlon, my first return to an Olympic event this year and I was keen to see how much I'd improved. The following weekend was the Bournemouth Olympic distance and then the weekend after that was Windsor Olympic.

My training was going really well. I had upped my running and was typically covering 25 to 35 miles a week. In the pool it was as if I'd grown fins. At the Triathlon Club I was told to move up two lanes. I was loving swimming now. Loving swimming, it's a twisted world. I was even developing a patchy sun tan. A month earlier I had been dressed ready for an Arctic crossing, now I was getting sunburnt on bike rides. Heaven. In my mind, this was the dream. I felt confident, fit and raring to go. As I was about to realise, I was walking a tightrope and it wouldn't take much to send me falling.

There was still the constant pressure. Three weeks earlier I had rolled my ankle running in the woods and I hadn't been able to run for two weeks. I divided my normal run sessions between cycling and swimming, but every day that I wasn't running, it gnawed away at me.

Sometimes I would feel so tired, drained and powerless. Every day Ironman Lake Placid got closer. Niggles ate away at my confidence.

Time was passing quickly. Days and weeks were merging. I would swim for an hour and my mind would be in the abstract, a rhythm, a blur. It was the same with cycling and running. Where had I been as the miles rolled by? All I had were snapshots and memories of routes in my mind, the warmth of the sun, the smell of the fields, sharp climbs and quick descents. I was stuffing down bananas, chewing Tracker bars, glugging sports drinks and worrying about my teeth. It was a great life and I was meeting some inspiring people. I met one guy, a very tall South African called Pete, who must have been in his late thirties, or maybe early forties. He was training for the Comrades Marathon, a gruelling double marathon in the searing heat of South Africa. He would run 80 to 90 miles a week. Hello? What was more, this was his tenth consecutive Comrades Marathon. He was delighted because success this year would ensure he got his Comrades number for life. He was living in an ultra athlete world. Happy and content, the troubles in his life blurred by his real passion. Pete was as cool as they come.

I, on the other hand, would lurch from being tired to feeling fresh. However, I'd never been fitter and it was time to put myself to the test over the next three races. First off was Milton Keynes Olympic Triathlon. Five days before the race Simon and I wisely went out for an open water swim at Brogborough Lake before we braved the muddy waters of Emberton Park, the venue of the triathlon. I learned an important lesson that day. I had to lose the shortie wetsuit. As Simon consistently pulled away from me I realised it gave me all the hydrodynamic qualities of a fully loaded oil tanker and had all the water retention qualities of a sponge. I also got bloody cold in it.

It was a warm, still, summer's evening. Simon and I gamely leapt in and set off for a buoy in the middle of the lake. Thirty seconds after my brave dive, I was back, knees blue, shivering on the shore. Simon, in his new 'Ironman' wetsuit was treading water, looking at me perplexed. After our first bike ride together in the snow I knew his tolerance of the cold to be that of a killer whale but this was ridiculous. He talked me back into the water and I spent 30 minutes trying to warm up in my shortie. I got out, cold to the core. My feet were marble white and even with two fleeces on and the heating in the car on full blast, it took the 20 minute journey home to get anything close to being semi-warm again. A cup of hot tea eventually quelled the shivers. But what worried me more than the cold was the fact that normally I was much quicker than Simon, yet I had been unable to prevent him from pulling away, clad in his new super-slick wetsuit. I needed no second opinion. The shortie had to go. I was lucky because Simon had bought two wetsuits the previous weekend with the intention of trying both, keeping whichever worked best for him and returning the other one. Now, although I would never admit this, we were both of a similar build, although I claim to be two inches taller and broader on the shoulder and slimmer on the waist. Simon therefore let me try on the spare Speedo wetsuit and I fitted into it like a glove. Sadly, the shortie would never race again.

Cautious to the end, two days later we returned to Brogborough and I realised why I had exited third from last in the swim at Windsor. In my new wetsuit I was almost planing as I skimmed across the surface of the water. Confident of exiting the swim ahead of me at Milton Keynes, Simon looked quite distressed that the advantage he had enjoyed two days previously had disappeared. Big lesson. If you're going to go open water swimming, go out and buy a good fitting triathlon specific wetsuit. It makes the world of difference.

All of a sudden I was really looking forward to the race on Sunday. As I have consistently demonstrated, my preparation for big events leaves something to be desired and this time was no exception. After some light training early in the week, I then took the Wednesday off. On Thursday it was a quick swim to ensure my new wetsuit was ship-shape, then I descended into the world of heavy metal. When I agree to these things I never really check the social calendar. On the Friday night Neil, Dave and I headed down to North London to see Motorhead play live. It was a great night, but one of the worst performances I have ever seen. I was back home and in bed by 1am. I know, not perfect, but I had stayed off the booze and out of the mosh pit. Remembering the lessons from Brighton last year, after the Reading Festival, I had erred on the side of caution this time. Oh well, I had the Saturday to recover, didn't I? No, not quite. It was the Oz Fest at the Milton Keynes Bowl. An all-day gig with some of the great metal bands of our time serenading us: Papa Roach, Tool (my personal favourite), Slipknot, Disturbed and not forgetting the legendary Black Sabbath. Definitely not the ideal taper. On the Saturday morning I got up early, cleaned my bike, mixed my drinks, got all my gear ready, then drove over to Emberton to register. I then sped back home, had a quick lunch and we were off. The metal fans assembled. Neil, (also racing on Sunday), Dave (not racing on Sunday) and I took the stroll from our house to the Bowl. Neil and I took it easy. Dave went for it. Neil and I, very sensibly limited ourselves to four pints each over the course of the afternoon. I know, real restraint. Not really rock and roll but the thought of Simon getting in the perfect preparation fortified my self-restraint. I couldn't let him beat me.

Again my head hit the pillow at 1am and I was ready for a good lie in. At 5.30am the alarm went off. 'Err, I am sleeping'. Beep, beep, beep. 'No, it's too early, I've just closed my eyes.' Beep, beep, beep. 'Where's the alarm?' I got up. Eyes glued half closed, mouth dry, confused and dazed. It was 5.30am. I had to race. 'Where is the bloody alarm?' This was the local triathlon. It would be certain humiliation in front of people I knew. To cap it all I'd had four and a half hours sleep. Slowly I was coming to. Finally I found the alarm. I washed my eyes, had the first of many pees, went downstairs and munched on a Tracker bar and a banana, the breakfast of champions. Okay, time for a bit of music to get me fired up, drink some tea, shave, drink more tea, finally my guts started to wake up. Go to the loo, shower, I was still on autopilot but slowly waking up. I dried off, dressed, congratulating myself on having the foresight to get everything ready the day before. I grabbed my bike from the garage and headed off in the car. It was 6.15am. I picked Neil up and we were in Emberton Park for 6.55am.

It was drizzling, grey and wet. I recognised people, said hello and had a bit of banter. I was wide-awake by now. Surreal really, given that Neil and I had been watching Ozzy only eight hours earlier. It was time to get down to business. I headed to transition to start getting ready. My routine was like a reflex now. I found a good spot for the Roo, memorising where it was, counted the racks, worked out where the swim would come in, where the bike would go out and return, and where the run would exit. With the Roo in place, I laid out my transition. This was now carried out with precision. Firstly a towel to stand on, my cycling shoes, straps loosened, talcum powder sprinkled inside. I then did the same with my running shoes. I placed my helmet upside down, front facing out with the chinstrap untangled and laid out on the outside of the helmet. I placed my sunglasses inside it. I'd switched to my orange lenses as the skies were grey. You've just got to love Oakley. I then fitted one large and one small drinks bottle to the bike, having learned from the previous year that one bottle was not enough. I even had a Lucozade drink sachet for the run, which I placed near my trainers. Oh yeah baby, this may be a local event but, putting Ozzy and Motorhead aside, I was racing my peers here. Pride and reputation were at stake. This was very, very serious.

I went to the loo one more time.

I was getting focused now. Sipping lager high on the banks of the Milton Keynes Bowl seemed a million miles away. There I was, early Sunday morning, in a freshly cut field, with a light drizzle, about to try and cover a 1 mile swim, a 25 mile bike ride and a 6 mile run as quickly as I possibly could. I was two months away from my first Ironman, with a winter of hard training behind me. I reasoned I had to be able to take this race in my stride, or I really did have something to worry about.

I pinned my numbers on and had a quick jog before the pre-race briefing. Then it was on with the new Speedo wetsuit, not forgetting the compulsory baby oil on my shoulders, neck, back, legs and arms to avoid rashes. As 8am grew closer, I headed to the start, zipped up my wetsuit, wet my face, tugged on my swim hat and goggles and lowered myself into the lake. I took a few strokes back and forth in the minutes before we lined up. The field assembled and the countdown to the gun began.

Four.

Three.

Two.

And there I was, for the first time ever, calm as a Hindu Cow, no nerves, following a routine that took me to the start gun.

One – Go!!!

Mayhem, surge of water. We were off. A confusion of black neoprene bodies. I held my water, swallowed a few mouthfuls of the lake, kicked, turned my arms, breathed and after a few frantic minutes it all settled down. When I rounded the first buoy, I looked back and half the field were behind me. On to the next buoy. My swimming line was terrible but I was keeping up. Despite zigging and zagging I stayed with the pack around the course. Mental note, next time I would start to the left of the pack and then I could take a bearing from them as I breathed to the right.

I put on a little surge as we rounded the last buoy and headed for the shore. Strong hands pulled me out. As I sped towards transition I pulled my goggles and hat off and started tugging my wetsuit down. My watch read 26 minutes. I was delighted. It spurred me on. I blinked and was out of transition. My leg went over the saddle, I clipped into the pedals, started my trip computer and moved my arms down onto the aerobars. The Roo increased speed and I worked up the gears. Me and the Roo. Off we went. I felt strong, my cadence felt fast and fluid. I knew the course. Simon, Neil and I had ridden it several times during the preceding weeks. The bike course flashed by, through villages, ascents and descents. Drink, change gear, watch for potholes, use the smooth bits of tarmac. I felt really good. Just over 1 hour and 7 minutes and I was climbing off the bike and running through transition to my rack. Shoes, helmet, glasses off. The trainers went on and I grabbed my drink sachet. Go. I looked at my watch. I knew I would do a personal best, but my speed over the next 6 miles would determine by how much. The run was three laps. The drizzle was now welcome, cooling me down. By now Linds and our friend Jane had arrived. Jane's husband, Matt, was racing in a team, doing the run section. It was great to see some friendly faces. The first lap was steady. My jelly legs after the bike ran themselves out after a few minutes. On lap two a Black Country Triathlon Club member cruised by in the infamous luminous strip. I latched on and picked up his pace, trying to hold him. I held the pace for a lap and a half, but started to hurt. I was running very close to my threshold. Gradually he pulled away but I kept him in sight and kept pushing. My legs were hurting but I held on, and there was the line. As I crossed it my head was spinning, my legs were aching, my heart was pounding and I was grinning from ear to ear. 2 hours, 15 minutes, 22 seconds. A personal best for the course and the distance. I had taken 7 minutes off last year's time. I was over the moon. As the adrenaline faded and the lactic acid tightened my muscles, the rain clouds rolled in. Simon, Neil and Matt finished shortly after. We had all had good races. We packed and left.

As Linds and I drove home I was chuffed. I felt invincible. Superman. Until I got home, that is. My legs stiffened quickly. My back was sore. I went to bed at 4pm and didn't stir until 7.30pm. Deep, blissful sleep. Motorhead, Ozzy and the Milton Keynes Triathlon had finally caught up with me. Bournemouth Olympic Triathlon was seven days away. I had two bowls of pasta and went to bed early.

On Monday I woke with aching limbs, a sore dry throat, and a sniffle. Hang on, Superman doesn't get colds. The cold ripened as the week went on. By Thursday I was doing my impression of the Marlboro Man again with a full, wake you up in the night 'work those abs' chest cough.

Hey, but still I reasoned, conning myself, I had done the Ballbuster with a cold so I would be fine for the Bournemouth Olympic Triathlon. I was kidding myself. The whole run up to Bournemouth was a hassle and I was doomed from the start. The race was on the Sunday so I travelled down on the Saturday. I felt terrible. Coughing and sniffing. Linds and I had just bought a second hand MGF convertible and I was in love with this little charcoal grey runaround. What better thing to do than take a run down to the coast? To complicate things even further I wanted to drop by and see an old University friend, James, who lived outside Southampton with his wife, Stephanie, and my godson, Alex. I had bought the coolest little bug car for him. Alex was four months old so the car, with a minimum age of nine months, was completely useless to him at the time, but when I get something into my head I have to do it. The problem was the box the car was packed in would only fit in the MGF if I had the roof down. I crammed my racing gear into the tiny boot and my Roo was on the back on a rack. I didn't feel right but I couldn't see the wood for the trees by this stage. In an open-top car, battling with rain showers, I wrapped up in as many layers as I could without jeopardising mobility too much and set off.

100 miles later with a freezing draft blowing down my neck and having only encountered two light rain showers, I pulled up outside their house. A worthy effort, I felt, for my godson. I spent a good couple of hours with the three of them catching up. James and Stephanie, both doctors, questioned my wisdom on hearing my gravelling, coarse, chesty cough. But hey, with only six years of study and five years practical medical experience each, what did they know? Again, wrapped up, roof up now, I continued on to Bournemouth.

On arrival I realised why you don't get many convertibles in the car parks of triathlon races. From the luxury of locking my bike safely in the boot of my Ford Mondeo Estate and doing all the necessary bits, I had to drag the Roo everywhere. Through packed halls, halfway into toilets, through the town centre, even into McDonalds to get some food. I felt terrible already and the love affair with the Roo was heading towards a painful divorce. After two hours of hassle I eventually settled in the hotel. From starting the day feeling run down and ill, I had magnified that and now felt tense and exhausted. Had I learned anything? Not yet. Like the Titanic, I continued to steam towards disaster.

After a quick shower I headed out to find the restaurant where I was meeting the guys from the Milton Keynes Triathlon Team, who were racing in the event. I coughed my way through the meal and headed off quite early. However, still no chance to rest. Linds had been to a Hen Party in London on the Friday night and Saturday so we'd decided she'd join me in Bournemouth by train on the Saturday night. What had seemed like a good idea when we had planned it weeks before, seemed very foolhardy now as I sat waiting for her train to arrive. To be honest, I still hadn't seen the pending disaster. I deluded myself with the 'Ballbuster with a cold' argument. I reasoned this would be a walk in the park, late night no problem. Hell last week I'd gone to Motorhead and Ozzy on consecutive nights and then enjoyed the race of my life. Me, I was bullet-proof. When my head hit the pillow at 12.30am I fell asleep immediately and slept soundly. Well, at least until my cough woke me. Fool.

The alarm sounded at 5.30am. If I thought I'd felt tired last Sunday, I now knew what tired really felt like. As I got ready my lungs continued to betray me and my nose streamed. I grabbed my gear and we headed to the start. Blue skies greeted us but it was still chilly. A cold northerly breeze stole any warmth away. I racked my bike and prepared my transition, worked out where the exits and entrances were and tried to relax. There was no calm Hindu cow today. My chest was tight and I felt jittery. As the start approached I pulled my wetsuit half on and went for a quick jog to calm what I thought were my nerves. Things just got worse. I was breathless. 10 minutes to go. I got my lucky kiss from Linds, pulled up my wetsuit and jumped down onto the beach. The sand felt cold underfoot. The race briefing started. Hang on a second, I hadn't even got in the water yet. The sequence wasn't right. I dipped under the start cord and plunged in. It was cold, clear and salty. I had a quick splash and returned to the briefing. Nothing felt right. I wasn't connected with what was happening. I hadn't adjusted to the conditions. Time was just moving too quickly.

The whistle went and we were off. We charged down the beach into the sea, knee deep, waist deep, dive forward, cold white surging water. Neoprene arms and legs all around me. Just swim. We rounded the first marker. We turned for the long straight. Things felt bad. My chest was tightening. I was breathless, powerless. Slow down, I coached myself, just pace yourself. I couldn't breathe.

I panicked. I stopped and treaded water. The pack moved away. Just relax I said to myself, get your breath. I tried to continue front crawling. Again, no air. My body just wasn't responding to my instructions. I stopped again, treading water. The last swimmer passed me. The pack was gone. I looked at the beach then back at the disappearing pack. A rescue canoe pulled up alongside me. The embarrassment. I held on, assuring the paddler I was alright, just a little panicked. The pack was in the distance, but I was determined not to let them go. I set off again trying to follow them. Pointless. I stopped, treading water again. It was over. I turned to the beach and swam in slowly. My feet touched the bottom, I stood, hat off, goggles off. I felt lost. I shouldn't be here. I couldn't believe what had happened. It was so quick, so final.

As I stood in the shallows I felt the sun on my face, warm and bright. I looked at my watch. 4 minutes. The seconds sped on. It had all happened in 4 minutes. Linds ran down to see if I was alright. How to describe my feelings? Inconsolable. I informed the Marshals that I had withdrawn, retrieved my bits from transition, went back to the hotel, showered, had breakfast and we watched the rest of the race. The sun warmed up but I just felt empty and broken. In retrospect, all things considered, my first DNF (did not finish) was inevitable. I shouldn't have shown up at Bournemouth in my state. Linds was absolutely great. I was sure the world would end that day. The sun was brilliant but I felt bleak and cowardly. The racing demons had come back. What if that happened at Lake Placid? All that effort for just 4 minutes of racing. All of a sudden I was very clear that I wasn't Superman. The confidence I had carefully built was shattered. As the days went on I reasoned and rationalised and vowed not to make the same mistake again. Looking back at Bournemouth and what happened, it was probably the best and richest lesson I learned in the whole year running up to Lake Placid. And as Ian Mayhew dryly pointed out, 'It's not all that bad. You were the first out of the water.'

The joke got funnier the further away I got from the beach.

Chapter 26

Bacon Butties

Now, let's just recap. What was my dumbest move? Entering this thing. What was my smartest move? Entering this thing. No time to brood over setbacks. Hell no, I had an Ironman to race. I'd taken a knock, but I couldn't just roll over and let the world take over. I had to dust myself down, get on my feet and just get going again.

A huge piece of advice here. If you want the motivation to do an Ironman, put the book down, grab your credit card, go to your PC, log on, pick a race and enter it. Pay your money and commit yourself. Once you're committed, you suddenly have a compelling motivation. After Bournemouth's DNF, I just had to get up and move on. I realised very quickly that I'd pushed myself too hard, set up races too close together and, inevitably, I had blown up. Once the disappointment had passed, I was so glad it had happened on the sunny south coast of England, rather than at 7.04am Eastern Standard Time July 29th 2001 in upstate New York. I realised I needed to ease off and recover, get better and get back to consistent training. I needed to pace myself. Heavy metal gigs, late nights and back-to-back racing had knocked me down. It was time to re-assess my plans and the race schedule. It didn't take a fortune teller to foresee the likely outcome of the next two races. Therefore, despite the £50 I'd sent to Human Race for my entry to the Windsor Olympic Triathlon, I decided to withdraw. This gave me three weeks to get in shape for the Weymouth Half-Ironman and then I had another four weeks from there to Lake Placid. With that simple decision made, I felt re-motivated and raring to go. Somehow, the pressure was off.

Firstly, I needed to recover. Now, I'm not saying I'm dumb, but when I put my mind to something, I can usually justify anything I want. At least it's a talent that comes naturally to me. Now the balanced individual, after such a debacle by the sea, would give themselves the best part of a week to recover. However, the race junky, endorphin addict, would create arguments about getting back on the horse. Guess which camp I fell into? As I rolled up in the car park of the Milton Keynes Duathlon summer race series, not two days after my aborted race, I promised myself that for the sake of my health I would treat it purely as a training event. I simply wouldn't race. I would keep my heart rate below 160 beats per minute. But honestly, have you ever really tried not to race when the start gun goes off and the field surges forward? It was a warm summer evening. In truth I had lined up with good intentions. I held myself back from the front row. The organiser called the words 'Marks, Set' and just before 'Go' I somehow found myself on the front row. Bang. We were off. Training my arse. Within two minutes my heart rate was 186bpm and I started trying to gain positions. To my credit, as I got to the bike I eased off a little. But then on the final run, it was taken out of my hands as some guy wanted to race me. He pulled up alongside and tried to pass. But I latched on. He would surge. I would stay with him. It was cat and mouse. There was no way I was going to let this go. We hit the last 500 metres and I went for it, pulling away. Over the last 100 metres I thought my chest would explode but I held him off. To be honest, I was the victim here. It's impossible not to race. The race had taken 45 minutes and whether it was sensible or not it had vanquished those demons again and restored my faith. I was smiling and Bournemouth was but a memory.

Work was busy for the rest of the week, which really was a blessing as it kept me from training. My cold cleared up and by the weekend I was back out on the bike. Over the next week I got back into the rhythm of hard work and steady training. I was focused on the Weymouth Half-Ironman. The Ironman had become more than a hobby. For the first time I wrote down a plan and worked out what I should be doing for the next seven weeks. I wished I'd done this eight months earlier.

But I was still tired and couldn't seem to shake it off. Out on my bike one Saturday I just got very hungry. It had been on my mind for a few weeks. Was I getting my diet right? I had been a vegetarian for 16 years but wasn't careful about planning what I ate. The effect of taking iron supplements the previous year had highlighted other potential shortfalls in my diet. I rode on still thinking about it. After the ride my mind was made up. I drove to my nearest Tesco superstore, went into the all-day café and had a bacon butty. I know, I know. The vegetarians will reel in horror at this point. This isn't an advert for eating meat. I believe you can do an Ironman as a vegetarian. But you need to take real care over your diet. I clearly wasn't. The outcome at Bournemouth had rocked me to my core. I had so much riding on this Ironman, I didn't want to take any chances. I would eliminate all risks. That night, Neil and I went out for a boy's night, a few beers and a Thai curry. I had spare ribs and chicken curry. I don't do things by halves. They tasted really good. Now, don't judge me, veggies. Ironman shouldn't be taken lightly. It influences everything in your life. It becomes a mechanism for prioritisation. You decide what's important and what's not.

The time rolled on. There were ups and downs. Weymouth was drawing close. A week before it I rolled my ankle running in the woods. Again, I just had to get up and dust myself down. I religiously iced my ankle and kept it elevated to get the swelling down. I would be racing a Half-Ironman in seven days. There was no time to mess around. I had to admit I was excited about Weymouth. Upping the distance would be a real test. By the end of the day, racing in anger, I would know whether I had the minerals for Lake Placid. Weymouth Half-Ironman would be the day I drew the line in the sand.

Chapter 27

Finding the Minerals

Have you ever had that sense of impending doom? Ever thought 'I know I haven't learned from my mistakes'? It was a beautiful sunny Saturday and we were heading to Weymouth to race my final outing before Lake Placid. Conventional wisdom would say, especially after a disastrous DNF, have a relaxed day, give yourself lots of time to get down to Weymouth, register, chill out, have an early meal, early to bed, and Bob's your uncle, you've never been so ready to race.

Ah. Now that would be conventional wisdom. Let me tell you why I was getting this sense of impending doom. We weren't going to Weymouth on Saturday. Oh no. We had opted for a more unconventional arrival in the wee small hours of Sunday morning. Instead of heading straight for Weymouth, we'd decided it would be best to go via Bath and Cardiff. To cut a long story short, we were scheduled to be at a friend's wedding in Cardiff. There was, however, a slight detour needed as I had to pick up my Roo from Bath where it had been residing with the importer who was sorting out some trouble I'd been having with the bottom bracket. So we hurtled into Bath - well, we queued for hours into Bath - I grabbed the Roo and we sped onto Cardiff for the wedding. It was like a scene from that infamous film. After numerous wrong turns and lots of swearing, we arrived at the church hassled and hot, three minutes after the bride, and had to sneak in at the back like naughty school children. It turned out to be a really enjoyable wedding and we pulled ourselves away reluctantly as the evening reception kicked off, to embark on the last 100 mile stretch of the journey to Weymouth.

Fortunately, with foresight, I had warned the B&B that we would be late. Still, I think they were surprised when we crept into our room at 1am. I quickly arranged my bits, we got into bed and fell fast asleep. There weren't any nerves that night. I was too tired.

As ever, it seemed as if I'd only just closed my eyes when the beep, beep, beep of the alarm penetrated my deepest dreams. Like a robot, I got up and started my routine. Tea, light breakfast, go to the loo. This was going to be the biggest race I had done to date: 1.2 mile swim, 56 mile bike ride and a half-marathon. Considering the memory of my last race and the previous day having been a nightmare, I was amazingly calm. We drove down to the start and met Nick, 'the unluckiest man in the world', who had kindly offered to register me for the race and collect my numbers the previous day. Everything hinted at disaster.

Now, if you are thinking of upping your distance, I would thoroughly recommend the Weymouth Half-Ironman, organised by conceptsport.co.uk. It is held in a great location and is a well run event. The start is about halfway down the seafront and the transition area is set up in some open air tennis courts above the beach. The swim course runs parallel to the seafront, up to a turn buoy, and then you swim back again. As you exit the water you cover a short stretch of beach, go up some steps and into transition. The bike route is a single loop course, all on incredibly smooth main roads. It is slightly rolling but, because of the road surface, the bike itself flies. The last 2 to 3 miles come down a long descent which enables you to ease your legs off for a two lap run course.

As I prepped my transition, the sun started to burn. I was really excited. It was going to be a classic day. Despite the antics of the day before, I felt great and raring to go. As I completed my warm-up jog I felt none of the tight chestedness or jitters of Bournemouth. Allowing plenty of time, I greased up with Vaseline and baby oil, pulled on my wetsuit and got into the sea for a warm-up swim. The water was warm. I felt a million miles from Bournemouth. Back on the beach I gave Linds a little kiss and headed for the pre-race briefing. We took our positions and the countdown started. I could feel myself smile. The calm Hindu cow was back.

And we were off on a running start. The pack surged into the water and we all quickly settled into the rhythm. As we headed down to the turn buoy, breathing to the right, I could see the seafront passing alongside me. Everything felt good. I was even overtaking people. We got to the top of the course, turned around the buoy and headed back.

And then all of a sudden, my feet touched the bottom and I was standing up. I saw Linds and she was yelling enthusiastically. I pulled off my goggles and hat as I waded out of the shallows and pressed the lap on my watch, 31 minutes. I looked back as I ran up the beach. Hang on, there were more people behind me than ahead of me. This wasn't normal. I sped up the steps, into transition and found my Roo. I was treating today as my final dress rehearsal for Lake Placid so, remembering Ian's advice 'the longer the race, the slower the transition', I was careful to take my time. I pulled off my wetsuit, washed my feet, took a glug from my energy bottle and pulled on my cycling shoes, helmet, gloves and sunglasses. I took another glug, loaded my pockets with Tracker bars and gels, grabbed the Roo and ran for the exit.

The bike route went down the front, through the town and headed east on the Bournemouth road. The Roo and I were flying along. My trip computer was showing a steady 20 mph. Was I going too fast? I kept on drinking and grazing. With no feedstations on the bike course I had four big bottles, two on the frame and two on the seat post cage. At the start this made the Roo heavy but to my relief it still shifted and I reasoned that, as the miles weakened my legs, the weight would reduce.

I nibbled away at a Tracker bar. I am always careful to put the wrappers in my back pocket. No matter how furious the race, don't litter the course. The route rolled on. The sun was getting stronger and the air warmer. I glugged on my drinks, nibbled my food, kept down on the aerobars and turned the pedals. Without a doubt, this was going to be a classic day. By the halfway mark I still felt really good. The Roo was flying, I had no back pain, I'd drunk two bottles so the bike felt lighter and I was lost in my own little world. I was talking to myself, checking I was alright, reminding myself to eat, urging myself on. It was a feeling I'll always remember, an eerie sense of tranquillity. As I got to the three-quarter stage, the bike route headed out towards the sea, continually rolling up and down hills. And then all of a sudden reality penetrated my isolated world as the hills disappeared and I descended towards Weymouth. The route in was fast and long and as the morning had progressed, traffic had built up with people heading for the sea, most completely oblivious to the fact there were bikes sharing the same road. So after a few near misses and close encounters with Neanderthal idiots intent on cutting me up, I played it safe, held my road and protected my braking distance. Also conscious of the fact that a half-marathon lay ahead of me, I ensured I had as much energy inside me as possible and as I neared the transition area I made sure that I'd squeezed every drop out of my bottles. I made a mental note – I'd stopped eating peanut bars at about the three-quarter mark to avoid cramps in my stomach. I'd planned to stop eating at this point but, coincidentally, I had lost my appetite for them as the day had grown warmer. I would have to be careful in Lake Placid, as I would still have another 60 to 70 miles to go and would need to keep on eating solids.

Down the seafront I flew and back into transition. I dismounted, stopped my trip computer and was lifted again as the display showed an average of 20.7 mph. For a hilly course I couldn't have hoped for more. As I racked my bike, my legs felt wobbly. Again, I coached myself, 'the longer the race…' I removed my helmet and glasses, took a long glug from my energy drink, removed my shoes and socks and pulled on some clean socks after carefully smearing my toes with fresh Vaseline. I put on a clean pair of sunglasses and set out with a small bottle of energy drink in my hand.

Now my legs *really* felt like jelly. All of a sudden, they felt like they'd cycled 56 miles. I pushed on, mindful of the fact that if I could manage to run a 1 hour 50 minute half-marathon, I could finish under the 5 hour mark. I jogged, I shuffled, pushing myself forward. The sun was getting high in the clear blue sky. With the warmth of the day, I drank continually from the bottle. The run was an anticlockwise loop which went out of Weymouth, through the suburbs, down a main road, through some more suburbs then back to the seafront. Obviously, that's quite an abbreviated version of 7 miles. To be honest it was just a blur. It hurt. It was hot. It was hard. The first lap fell behind me and as I passed through the halfway point, I saw Linds. She'd missed me coming in on the bike, claiming afterwards she hadn't expected me back so soon. I could forgive her with comments like that. I gave her my now empty bottle and shuffled on. I can't remember what I said to her but apparently it didn't fill her with confidence. She worried about me for the next lap. It was funny; the run was living hell, my legs were sore and they ached, my back was stiff and my energy reserves felt very low, the sun beat down relentlessly, but all that aside, I was absolutely loving it.

I looked at my watch and realised I could break 5 hours. Again, my spirits lifted. No, I don't remember the pain subsiding much, but I pushed on. For me this was what it was all about. Here I was pushing myself to the limit, going beyond what I knew I could do. As I shuffled around Weymouth I was getting to know myself. I was having to look inside and ask the question, 'go on or slow down?' I kept on asking more of myself and, as the minutes sped towards the 5 hour mark, I kept on giving more, I kept on racing. Despite the pain, I urged myself on. I even started to stretch my stride out and tried to go faster over the last 3 miles.

I pounded on, glancing nervously at my watch. Eventually the finish line arrived and the clock read 4 hours, 56 minutes. I was over the moon. I had run the half-marathon in 1 hour 46 minutes, just 13 minutes slower than my run at Great Barford the previous December. I assured Linds I was fine. She scolded me, telling me how she was wracked with anguish from my comments at halfway. In truth, I was on cloud nine. The demons from Bournemouth had evaporated. I now knew I was ready for Lake Placid. Okay, so it was double the distance, but I wouldn't race so hard. I was ready.

Racing at Weymouth had been a new experience for me. Racing for five hours was very different from the somewhat furious races I was used to. Over five hours I'd had far more time for reflection. I'd looked deeper inside and asked myself harder questions. Time had moved into a different dimension. I had been in my own private cocoon, intimate and alone. It had been captivating.

We packed up and headed into the countryside to find a pub serving food. Sitting in the pub garden over a pint of Guinness and a pint of water, I felt a million miles from the darkness of Bournemouth. I couldn't believe the step change in me from when I'd sat sweating in the garden reading Pete Goss' book, frustrated at only being an armchair adventurer. From reading about others facing hardship and challenges, I was now pushing myself beyond what I considered to be normal behaviour. I was forcing myself to check my metal, see whether I had the minerals, asking myself the question 'go on or stop?' I smiled. Today had been a good day.

Chapter 28

The Roo Is Dead

A sad, sad, day. I'd had visions of me and the Roo climbing to glory, battling, attacking the course, racing in the high peaks of upstate New York. Me and my black steed, soaring, climbing, ah the victories. Alas, four weeks before the big event, the Roo met its maker. The Roo is dead. Long live the Roo.

Then again, praise be to the lycra-clad guardian that it was the Roo and not me. I'll be forever indebted. Whilst my bike disappeared under the car, I sailed over the bonnet. But let me tell you the full story.

Having raced well at Weymouth, my confidence was restored. It was Monday night and time for a recovery ride. It was warm. So warm that I almost left my helmet in the car at the gym. But as I was about to close the boot, I thought better of it, a decision that probably saved my life, given the dent in the front of my now useless helmet and the impact I took on my face. I set out to do the Milton Keynes Triathlon bike circuit towards Olney. I did one lap and felt strong, so I decided to do a second. I was going well. Down on my aerobars, my legs felt as if nothing would stop them. The Roo was racing on, wanting to go faster. Three roundabouts from the gym, I was low on the aerobars, trying to edge up the average speed. I checked to my right. All clear. I headed into the roundabout, held my line, my right of way. On my left I saw a black Ford Sierra coming in on the next entrance, going fast. I clocked him, he seemed to be slowing, looking at the traffic, so I didn't give him a second thought. I pressed my pedals and continued the line towards my exit.

Bang. Metal on metal. A hammer blow on my left leg. Breaking glass. Black bonnet below me. Flying up in the air. Then I felt the road.

My face hit the tarmac first, forehead, nose, chin, followed by right elbow, right hip. Then silence. At that moment, the moment I hit the road, the depth of my obsession became clear. My only thought was 'Oh no, Ironman'.

'You're in the middle of the road. You'll get hit again. Get up, get to the verge'. I stood and hopped to the verge, unable to put weight on my left leg. I laid down and curled up in searing pain. The car had hit me side on. I was numb. I couldn't believe I'd been hit by a car. I lay in a ball, shocked, helpless, full of disbelief. I was in a lot of pain and must have passed out. I remember coming round and hearing voices but all I could see was my bloodied curled hand in front of my tingling face. People were around me. A coat had been laid over me. A guy was crouched down beside me, a PE Instructor from the Milton Keynes prison and he was speaking to me. He asked me questions and assured me that I was alright. It kept going over in my mind, 'I've been hit by a car. Lake Placid is only four weeks away. My left ankle must be broken, my legs are bust. I won't be able to go.'

That thought was almost worse than the pain.

A woman's voice spoke to me asking for a number to call. Linds had a job that covered a good part of the country and was away for the night with work. I couldn't remember her mobile number off the top of my head, as it was quick dial on my phone. Neil's was the only number I could remember. They called an ambulance and kept talking to me. Time stood still. I was helpless and people were helping me. I couldn't move. I could really only see my bloodied hand. I was in shock. The ambulance arrived. The police were there. I felt a neck brace go around my neck and I was strapped to a table.

Jackie's face came into view, then Neil's. Familiar faces. I smiled.

'How's my bike? My sunglasses came off. I don't know where my heart rate monitor is.'

'Don't worry, we'll get them', they reassured me.

I only found out later that Neil had gone into a state of panic as they drove up, seeing the ambulance and the police. When I heard, I imagined my panic if it had been the reverse, seeing Neil, one of my best friends, lying on the road. That's when friendship really counts. They had taken the call, left their supper just out of the oven and raced over. Not a second thought.

As I lay there bloodied, knocked and numb, head and neck fastened in a brace, strapped to a stretcher board, I felt a warmth come back into my body when I saw their faces appear in the sky above me. I wasn't alone.

The paramedics lifted me into the ambulance, Jackie climbed in, closed the door and we were off. Neil followed behind in the car. Jackie and I were joking now. She was seven and a half months pregnant with twins. All in all, the paramedics were more interested in how she was. They took my pulse, about 72 beats per minute. I was annoyed it wasn't lower. The shock was starting to pass. Neil called Linds on the way to the hospital. She was 100 miles away and went into a state of shock with Neil's opening gambit of 'I don't want to worry you but are you sitting down?' Good old Neil, don't go into trauma counselling, unless you are trying to create trauma.

At Northampton hospital all the staff were fantastic. They checked me out. No spinal injuries, amazingly no broken bones, just bruises, cuts, gravel rash and grazes. A nurse cleaned and bathed the cuts. I looked at my face in the mirror. It looked like someone had taken to it with a cheese grater. A cut on my forehead, grazing down my nose, a black and bloodshot eye. I looked at my cracked helmet and saw the big dint in the front. I shuddered to think what could have happened without it. Thank you Giro. I had deep cuts on both elbows, my hands were bloodied, my hips and legs were grazed and bruised, with big holes in both knees. My back was cut and feeling very tender.

Now in hospital, with professional medical staff around me, the shock that I'd been knocked off my bike by a car started to subside. I was laughing and joking and wincing as the nurse cleaned my cuts and grazes. As I came back to my senses, I started to become aware of the fact that I stank. And you know it's bad when you can smell yourself. The nurse was very polite but Neil and Jackie didn't hold back. As we laughed I felt better and better. To give the guy who hit me credit, and I credit him very little for his driving skills, he called the hospital to check I was okay and to say he was sorry. Despite potentially shattering my Ironman dreams, this call of concern went a long way to help me forgive him. But please drivers, look twice for bikes.

My head throbbed. Assured that nothing was broken, I didn't want to spend the night in hospital. I was determined to walk out. So I did. Well, limped. I spoke to Linds and reassured her I was fine. She was a long way away. She had taken the call about 8.45pm from Neil and had been in a pub with colleagues drinking. Neil had very sensibly told her under no circumstances to try and drive home and that they would look after me. I looked in the boot of Neil's car and there was the Roo, a distorted mess. The car had gone over it, dragging it along as it died. That Monday night ride around the Milton Keynes Triathlon circuit was tragically the last flight of the Roo.

What would I do about the Ironman?

Neil and Jackie put me up for the night, but only on the condition that I had a shower. That shower really hurt as the water ran over every cut and graze, but at least the smell disappeared. For revenge, I bled on their sheets and pillows all night. True friends.

I got up late the next day. My head thumped, really thumped. Every part of me hurt but I had loads on at work, so headed in just to sort things out. As I walked into the office in a pair of old shorts and a polo shirt borrowed from Neil, the 'what are you wearing?' jibes and feigned outrage turned to silence as my colleagues saw my face, arms, hands and legs. Did I look that bad? My head still throbbed. I sorted out the essential bits of work, then went round to the police station to give my statement. When I walked in, the policemen already knew all about it. One of the guys there was a member of Milton Keynes Triathlon Club, so I got an extra warm welcome. They assured me they had witnesses, it was very clear cut. The driver's insurance details were fine, he was taking responsibility. I limped out. Time to replace the Roo.

I headed for my favourite shop, Phil Corley Cycles. Now Phil, who I know well, saw a sales opportunity as I limped in, crumpled Roo in hand. And I'm a sucker for a deal. First things first. New helmet and new heart rate monitor. Okay, what about a bike? Now, how Phil does his magic I don't know but I got a fantastic deal. I got the bike of my dreams and he got way more money than I intended to spend. I don't begrudge him. Far from it. He sold me exactly what I wanted and had dreamed about. It would take a few days to be ready. I was limping. I couldn't straighten my right arm and my brain felt about five times too big for my skull. What was a few days?

As I drove away, despite my despair and hurt, my dark feelings and loss of hope for Lake Placid, I had an excited knot in my stomach. I needed to repair myself as quickly as possible and I knew that as I healed myself over the next 48 hours, a brand new carbon fibre Trek 5200 was being prepared for me. It was the same frame Lance Armstrong had won the 2000 Tour de France on. With that sales pitch, I hadn't stood a chance. I was delighted. I went home and had another torturous shower. Every time the water touched my cuts my eyes watered. I was numb by the end with sickening pain. As I writhed in the shower, Linds popped her head around the corner, looked me up and down and had to lie down on the floor to stop herself from fainting, feeling dizzy, sick and queasy all in one. Did I look that bad?

If I felt despair after Bournemouth, it was nothing compared to this. I was so close and had put so much into this dream, I was determined to get better. Over the next two days my spirits bounced from low to lower. Sleeping was no fun. Limping was no fun. I couldn't straighten my right arm. I felt empty. I planned to race an Ironman in less than four weeks, something I had dedicated the last 12 months to. After the Half-Ironman at Weymouth I had never felt more ready. I had paid for flights, entry and accommodation. We had everything planned. All that work, worry and effort for nothing. My dreams had evaporated in a split second. That was my darkest moment. I didn't know what to do. I'd come to a stop. I was shattered. All I could do was what I'd done for the last year. Whenever I had come up against an obstacle, I would find a way around it and just keep going.

Now my Mum has a theory that through some telepathic link she has with me, she knows when I am hurt or ill. I have always had my doubts about this telepathy. And to be honest, Mum's behaviour after this crash did nothing to confirm her 'supernatural' powers and did a lot to reinforce my already healthy scepticism. There was no call. No e-mail. Nothing. Telepathy, my arse. Eventually I called her.

'Do you know, I knew there was something wrong.' Oh, here we go.

'Well, why didn't you call?'

'I was going to. You know, I had a dream.'

'Oh, come on Mum.'

'I did' (her voice got louder, more insistent.)

I was smiling again. Telepathy or not, mums make sons feel better. At least mine does.

I had four weeks to the Ironman. Well, 23 days in fact. I would do the race. I just had to find a way. After work the following day, I went back to Phil Corley's to try two frame sizes for my Trek. I rode up and down the street outside his shop a few times. My knees were stiff, my arms tight. I was still unable to straighten my right elbow, but it felt good to be pedalling again. My heart raced whenever I saw a car. With cuts raw and exposed, a face and head all bruised and swollen, I felt very vulnerable. The 54 centimetre frame it would be. My new weapon of choice. If you want to buy a decent bike, go and see Phil Corley. He and the guys there provide a great service and really know their stuff. Phil, happy to have helped me find the bike of my dreams, also offered to transfer all my recoverable bits from the Roo. My new Trek would be ready the following day.

Happy that I was moving forward, getting back on track, I headed down to the gym for a swim. Well, a bob more than anything. I reasoned the water would help ease any injuries. Before getting in the pool I walked slowly for 30 minutes on the treadmill. Regulars at the gym, used to seeing me pound out the treadmill and grind out endless spinning sessions, would stop and look at me walking, pausing at the machine as if about to ask, then see my face, arms and legs and decide against the question.

I changed and went through to the pool. Getting in was agony. My cuts still felt raw. Front crawl was out of the question. With a black eye and cuts down my face, wearing goggles was a big no no. I grabbed a float and kicked up and down for six lengths (150 metres) then got out. Time to call Mum again to get cheered up.

How was I going to recover in 23 days? This wasn't fun anymore. It was the middle of summer, sticky hot and uncomfortable in a suit. Perfect training weather and I could do nothing. Time was ticking away.

I went into London the following day. I had lost my smile again after another restless night. I dodged people on the tubes, wincing every time someone got close. I had to get better and I had to get my arm straightened. On the train back I called a sports injury clinic in Milton Keynes, the Blackberry Clinic, and made an appointment for that afternoon.

And that afternoon, the tide that had gone out so far started to come back in. On the way across for my treatment I'd picked up my new Trek. I now had a vehicle. In the foyer I assured the Receptionist, who took one look at my face and was convinced I had been in a fight, that I was a peace loving ex-vegetarian. The Blackberry Clinic is run very well and I was lucky enough to get a physiotherapist called Rochelle. (The fact her name was Rochelle wasn't the lucky bit.) Rochelle was a Kiwi, over here working with her husband who was an ex-triathlete. I explained my plight to her, she looked me over and said 'Of course we can fix you.' Music to my ears.

Now I am a great believer in the power of the mind. If an expert tells you you're alright, even if you're not, you'll heal much quicker. With that one piece of reassurance, the lights came on, hope rushed in and the clouds rolled back. Now the next 45 minutes were quite painful. I'll spare you the details but needless to say I walked out with a straightened arm. I am forever indebted to Rochelle. She was probably about five feet tall but she didn't let her size get in the way. Despite her slight frame I think she would have given Hulk Hogan a run for his money. She assured me that low-intensity cycling was fine, (which was lucky given that I had a date with my new Trek 30 minutes later), and swimming would be great when my arms felt stronger. But for the moment running was a big no no. I positively skipped out of the Blackberry Clinic. My spirits were high. If Rochelle said I'd be fine, that was enough for me. What was more, I had a new bike. And not just any bike. I had my dream bike, Lance Armstrong's bike.

I got home and went for a test ride. It was perfect. It just seemed to accelerate. I was still jittery, in fact very jittery with cars around, but I was back. They built a tough chassis, I told myself. I had restored my hope. Okay, I couldn't swim or run and in 22 days I would have to cover 2.4 miles in the water and 26.2 miles on foot. But they were minor details.

Linds came home to a happier man, although she did shatter some of my illusions when she told me the Trek, in her humble opinion, felt heavier than the Roo.

Women. Yes, your bum *does* look big in that.

Chapter 29

Weebles Wobble...

I had finished work and was standing in our back garden, dressed in shorts, sandals and a T-shirt, my hands greased with oil, my new Trek in pieces at my feet. We were flying to Lake Placid the following day. The last three weeks had been a whirlwind. I had no idea how I'd done it but I'd picked myself up. Faced with the choice 'Stop or go on?' I had opted without a second thought to press on. Here, in our garden, where all this had started, I stood over the various pieces of my bike, praying I would be able to remember how they all fitted back together.

Straight after the crash, Rochelle had helped me enormously. Her reassurance that, in her succinct, professional opinion, 'we can get you fixed up', with a slight Kiwi accent, had filled me with hope. And she didn't pull any punches on the treatment table, yanking me this way and that, massaging tender muscles, remobilising stiff joints and sticking acupuncture pins into me to activate nerves. I was amazed at how she sped up my recovery.

The Trek was like a dream to ride. When I pushed the pedals, it flew. Admittedly it hadn't transformed me into a Lance Armstrong, but it was still phenomenal, exhilarating. As we cruised along my familiar routes, the frame and wheels would hum efficiently below me and with the slightest hint of increased effort, I could feel it accelerate from underneath me. The frame felt so light and the bike just absorbed any bumps and jarring on the road. It was a joy. In the ten days after having picked it up from Phil Corley's I'd ridden 250 miles, initially nervous and tentatively easing the stiffness from my knees. My heart would race as I went through roundabouts, fixing approaching drivers with my stare. As the aches subsided and my joints eased off I upped the mileage and the effort. I was back to evening rides outside in the cooling heat of the summer day.

However despite the overall smoothness of the Trek, I still hadn't got the setup right and couldn't get comfortable on the aerobars. My neck and back would ache after rides. But I would keep on fiddling with the dimensions. I knew I would find a solution.

I'd also got back on track with my swimming. After my initial aborted effort at a swim, a miserable six lengths kicking with the float, Rochelle had urged me to use my arms, once she had pulled and twisted them back to full mobility. Faced with the realisation that swimming was far less painful than 40 minutes with her, I headed for the pool. Again I started slowly but my spirits were lifted massively when, through gritted teeth, I managed to slog out 2.4 miles. Two weeks after the accident being able to knock out the distance again was a big relief. Admittedly, I hadn't quite figured out how I would fare with my wetsuit rubbing against the cuts on my knees and elbows, but I reasoned I'd cross that bridge at the appropriate time.

My running had taken a little longer, mainly because I'd taken the full brunt of the car on my left knee. In Rochelle's humble opinion, the fact that at the time I did very little stretching before or after training, ironically went a long way to preventing more damage. (I don't advocate this incidentally. I am now a religious stretcher.) Uncharacteristically for me, I didn't want to aggravate damage through foolhardy stupidity, so I waited a full two weeks and then gingerly stepped out to run 5 miles. To my great relief, my left knee felt fine. But afterwards my right quad, just above the knee, felt as if someone had stabbed me with a hot knife. Undeterred, I stretched and stretched and stretched. Two days later I ran again, this time covering 10 miles. Once more, I was cautious in the extreme, stopping to stretch each quad every 15 minutes. This time they felt fine. Physically I was back. Okay, so my Ironman preparation had taken a slight blip. Ideally it would have been nice to have finished Weymouth, enjoyed a gentle couple of weeks recovery and then built up to Lake Placid. But despite the unexpected turn of events, I knew as I stood in our garden that, with a fair wind, I would finish the Ironman.

Looking back, those last three weeks whacked me out mentally. At first I wasn't aware of it, but with all the emotion, effort, determination and uncertainty I had become twisted up inside on the nerves and tension. For the first 10 days after the crash I had continually woken throughout the night in a cold sweat. As our departure date had got closer, I'd wanted my recovery to get quicker. Slowly I'd become so wound up inside that I was restless, sweaty and having strange dreams. A little imbalanced, I decided it was time to stop taking the anti-inflammatory tablets and instantly the dreams and sweats stopped and I was sleeping again. But until I was back running and swimming I was a bundle of nerves. It was time for the Hell's Angel, heavy metal, wild man to re-establish the equilibrium, and my alter ego did it the only way it knows how. It was five days before our departure to America and we went to see Robbie Williams play live at the Milton Keynes Bowl. Since we lived only a short walk from the Bowl, all our friends, and anyone we vaguely knew who wanted to park their car outside our house, had come round for a BBQ beforehand. Linds had the lack of foresight to position me as bartender and chief grill man. Both positions I took to with great gusto and energy. Very soon we had quite a party atmosphere, and to ensure I was the most genial of hosts I drank and drank all afternoon, continuing the binge right through the concert. Falling, literally, into bed at 2am with the room spinning faster than a fruit machine, I remember feeling ashamed at my lapse. However, in retrospect, it had been exactly what I'd needed at the time. The perfect Neanderthal therapy for pushing the accident right out of my mind.

I woke early the next day, pulled out my bike, gritted my teeth and, with my head throbbing, sweated out the booze for two hours. That afternoon we headed to the Proms in London as Linds' mum, Lynne, was singing at the Royal Albert Hall. Sitting there in the Balcony was slightly cathartic. Let's put it this way, it was warm, and any alcohol I hadn't sweated out in the morning I slept off whilst being serenaded by the Proms. I wasn't the only one mind you. I could hardly hear the music over Linds' dad's snoring.

With the accident, Robbie, the booze and the Proms behind me, I went back into work for the last few days before heading out to Lake Placid. On the final afternoon, Jules, a friend at work, had organised a great surprise. When I got back to my desk after lunch, it was covered with useful bits for the race. There was a rubber ring, fins, a mask and snorkel, a can of 'Alligator Repellent' (no I still hadn't watched the film 'Lake Placid'), a Barbie drinks bottle, a child's cycling helmet, some stabilizers, a toy ambulance and some blister tape. Jules had also organised a cake and card. I was really quite moved.

We'd also managed to raise £2,250 in pledges. Jules, self-appointed Campaign Manager, had single-handedly twisted everyone's arm to cough up. I had meant to keep it low key but was actually really glad we were raising money. (I chose Cardiomyopathy, a heart disease charity, as the cause.) With all their best wishes I left work.

Now all that faced Linds and I was the journey and a very long day. I was happy there in our garden. Happier in myself than I had been in a long time. I knew I was about to realise a dream. A dream I had bent my will towards for the last 12 months. Linds and I were about to fly thousands of miles to do something I had thought impossible. Something I had considered to be insane. I think Linds was still having those thoughts. I felt a certain calm. Life had never been richer. I had never felt more alive.

PART 4

Eastern Standard Time

Chapter 30

Stateside

I adjusted my watch as the plane taxied to the terminal at Montreal Airport. If I ever thought the build up to the Ironman was intense, all of a sudden I could feel every minute pulsing. The flight had been a breeze. My big red bike bag had gone effortlessly into the hold. We had boarded and settled down for the six-hour flight. Conscious of not getting dehydrated, I had two 1.5 litre bottles of water. Both were empty by the time we entered Canadian airspace, and my continual trips to the toilet had earned me some very worried looks from fellow travellers. By the end of the flight I was fairly confident that I wasn't dehydrated.

The plane touched down in Canada in the early evening, so we had opted to stay at one of the airport hotels and pick up our hire car the following morning and journey to Lake Placid. Hoping for a cosy Canadian lodge, we were somewhat surprised to find our particular choice had a personality rating of zero. It was about as homely as a prison. But despite the brown retro décor, the dry air and lack of service, it was clean. With the flight behind us and our combined nerves, we were ready for a meal and an early night.

However, like synchronised swimmers, we woke simultaneously as comatosed sleep transformed into bug-eyed insomnia at 3am. We both lay there staring at the ceiling, wide awake courtesy of our jet lag. For the next three hours we read, talked, watched crass Canadian/American sit-coms, and read some more. Time moves really slowly between 3am and 6am. The personality shortfalls of an airport hotel are magnified yet further between these times as the world wakes in an eerie light. So at the earliest possible point we headed down to breakfast. Full, we returned to the room, picked up our already packed gear, checked out and headed for the car hire desk. The already long day wasn't going our way as, to our dismay, we were an hour too early to collect the car. So we circumnavigated the block a few times, read some more and headed back to the desk at opening time. All this time with a huge red bike bag in tow, stacked high on a baggage trolley. It wasn't even 9am yet it felt like we had been awake almost a full day.

Eventually the desk opened, we got our keys and headed down to the parking 'lot' to find our transportation. There she was, 'moored up' in the middle. Neither of us had realised we had hired a small pleasure cruiser on wheels. There she lay in front of us, a huge, long, green, immaculate Lincoln. The car was so big that even though it was a saloon the bike bag could be laid flat in the 'trunk' and there was room to spare. Linds was nominated helmsman / driver and I was navigator / first mate of the good green ship Lincoln. I cast off and we set sail, playing with the air con, heated seats, auto CD changer, cruise control, electric seat adjusters and any other gadgets we could find.

Maybe it's me, but distances in the States seem to quadruple when you're driving them. My calculations on our ETA in Lake Placid were quickly amended to the time we would reach the US border, and then revised again to when we would leave the Montreal city limits. The place is vast. We sped along, mindful of the draconian speed limits. After an age we arrived at the border of the 'Land of the Free' and passed through fairly quickly. My answer to 'Reason for visit?' I thought was fairly cool, 'Racing Ironman Lake Placid'. However, the border guard didn't seem to grasp the significance and, wishing to stay on his better side, I decided not to challenge him on his lack of awe.

On route I was keen to get some of the race's official energy drink so we stopped at a clean and impersonal shopping mall, though to give the mall credit it was positively vibrant compared to our airport hotel. America is also the land of the consumer, and they *do* consume. With drink in hand we fled from the air-conditioned hell and ran for the hills.

The road rolled on and on, and eventually we pulled off the freeway and started to wind our way through the foothills, forests and growing mountains, heading up to the 'Ski Station – Lake Placid'. Ski station, I didn't recall them advertising that fact too heavily on the Ironman website. The foothills quickly transformed into mountains, with ski lifts, cliffs, crags, fast-flowing rivers and gullies. It was breathtaking but the beauty was somehow lost behind the 'I am racing up here' thoughts.

Our accommodation for the stay was incredibly glamorous. With no expense spared, we had booked a motel about seven miles outside the town of Lake Placid. Although Linds didn't say anything I think she was very impressed by the 360 degree wood panelling in our room and the trinket and furry ornament shop that doubled as a reception. It wasn't unnerving in the slightest. We could almost hear the banjos in the background. We checked in, unpacked and headed into town. Again the drive up was spectacular but my nerves were growing the higher we drove. Maybe I should have read the course profile in more detail. It transpired that the distance from our motel to Lake Placid corresponded exactly to the final seven mile climb of the bike course. As we cornered each bend I was thinking 'this must be it, the end', only to see the route go up and continue ahead of us. Eventually we arrived and as we parked on the outskirts of town I felt a little shell-shocked. Again, I didn't remember them pushing that climb too actively when they took my registration fee and credit card details.

With wide streets, affluent housing and the stars and stripes fluttering from every flagpole, Lake Placid is your typical all America 'High School, Apple Pie, I love Uncle Sam' town. With traditional alpine wooden clad buildings, you couldn't find a nicer spot to take a holiday. It was the Wild West, meets American Sweetheart, meets The Shining. Too long here would certainly push me over the edge.

The 'Ironman Village' was set up on the sports field of the local high school. As we walked in through the crowds, we could feel the energy and anticipation. It was thrilling. We could sense the pent up excitement and nerves of those milling about. Despite my cool English reserve, I was immediately swept up in it and loving the buzz. I left my bike in one of the bike mechanic service tents for a final check over and to ensure nothing had been damaged during the flight. After a few laps exploring the Ironman Village, we headed back into town to find a pasta restaurant.

Walking up the main drag we couldn't help but be impressed with the setting. Lake Placid Ironman is set in and around a town called Lake Placid. The town hugs Mirror Lake and as we looked out from the main High Street, the lake was absolutely still, crystal clear, with the swim course buoys stretching out from the jetty. The buoys marked the start and followed the course out to the turn point and back down closer to the town, to the swim exit. It was a two lap swim course. Even looking at 1.2 miles, it seemed a long way. Beyond Mirror Lake the view rolled away from the far shore, green tree clad hills running up to a mountainous skyline, offset on blue skies with a setting sun. It was all I had dreamed about.

Hand in hand, we wandered through the town soaking up the atmosphere until we found a restaurant. My sympathy for Linds grew as conversation in the restaurant was almost exclusively centred around triathlon. But she had her revenge as, much to my dismay and to her pleasure, everyone thought she was the one racing. She still mentions it to this day.

As darkness fell and the temperature plummeted we headed back to the car and drove the descent back to our motel. It had been a long day from our 3am start back in Montreal and as soon as our heads hit the pillow we were fast asleep. Well, until five hours later when we were both staring bug-eyed at the somewhat scary wooden clad ceiling of our motel room.

Chapter 31

Final Two Days - The Devil's In The Detail

There we were, on the other side of the Atlantic, in a motel room at the bottom of a mountain that I would be racing up twice. These last two days were all about the finishing touches. The days passed slowly, but all the time I was aware of pending adventure. Time crept forward and as it did my nerves and adrenaline bubbled away inside. We headed into the town of Lake Placid to make the final preparations. First stop, had my Trek survived the flight? To my relief it passed the check with flying colours.

I was still in two minds on whether to use the aerobars. My back was still feeling stiff and I couldn't get used to the subtle change of position after the Roo. In the Ironman Village I saw some half-inch aerobar raiser blocks, so I put these on the bike and gave it a try. These little wedges fit inside the clamp attaching the aerobars to the frame and essentially raise the height of the aerobars. Everything seemed fine. The blocks created an unusually high riding position, which made me look as if I was riding a shopping basket clad bike, but any concerns about trying to remain cool seemed insignificant. My only concern was finishing the race. Over the years I have actually weaned myself off these blocks, mainly because of the ridicule from Neil and Simon, but there at Lake Placid I would take the taunts. The aerobars were staying on.

All this fiddling, worrying and tweaking was done in the rising heat of the day. Unperturbed by my constant search for the next portaloo, I knew I had to keep hydrated, so relentlessly I kept on drinking. In accordance with the laws governing one's perceived passage of time in relation to one's desire for time to speed by, time was moving very slowly. I was mindful of not wearing myself out, pre-warned that if I rushed around like a fool getting endless bits ready, by the time the gun went off I would be exhausted. We had no need to rush; we had time on our side. But even taking it slowly was difficult, it was just so unfamiliar. I was so used to filling every moment of every day with action, that suddenly being aware of the need to chill slowed the passage of time even further.

I wanted to do a quick trial of half the swim course. I felt nervous, as I hadn't been in my wetsuit since the Weymouth Half-Ironman and although my joints were healed after the accident, I still had scabs and grazes on my elbows and knees. To allay my fears I wanted to get a feel of what I had to worry about swimming with all the friction on them. So, under the cooling shade of a tree by Mirror Lake, I covered myself in Vaseline and baby oil and eased on the wetsuit.

Still really unsure of what to expect as I waded out into the water, I was relieved to discover that Mirror Lake was invitingly warm. It was clean, clear and refreshing. When the water was waist deep I dived forward and started to front crawl. Slowly the right bank slipped behind me. It was a long straight and eventually I reached the top of the course. I rounded the two turn buoys and headed back. The sun shone brilliantly, the air was a comfortable 28 to 30 degrees and the water was glorious. As I cruised along I felt a million miles from my first panic-struck open water swim in Brogborough Lake. I looked down into the deep nothingness between breaths and tried desperately not to think of the mythical Lake Placid crocodile. To my relief, when I pulled my wetsuit off, safe on the bank, free of reptile bites or even sightings, my fears of the scabs causing me problems disappeared. They had softened in the water and with the rubbing I was just left with bright pink skin on all my corners.

Having allayed at least some of my fears, we had a slow lunch and then headed into town as I needed to replace my sunglasses. I quite reasonably believed I'd be able to lay my hands on some cheap Oakleys, based on the fact I was in a town hosting an Ironman and we were in the States, after all, the spiritual home of Oakley wrap-around shades. But to my dismay, Lake Placid isn't the sunglasses capital of the world. In fact, the choice on offer in town made a UK petrol station forecourt's selection look impressive. On this huge point, you will be relieved to know I eventually found a black pair. Be warned. 'Shades Poker' is a high stakes game and you lose at your peril. To be frank it makes 'T-shirt Poker' look like snap next to five card stud. Or again, maybe it was all in my mind.

With the Ironman preparation out of the way for the day, we headed off in our small cruiser, the good ship Lincoln, to a local town where we stopped by another lake to take some time out from the bustle of Ironman, grab an ice-cream and read our books. Time had virtually frozen. With impending action so close, the wait was nerve-racking and exhilarating at the same time. We laughed, we joked, we tanned, we waited. In retrospect and with more experience, I should have done a little more over this period, just to keep fresh. I was tapering but also getting lethargic. I should have done a quick 30 minute jog, just to get the heart going. As the temperature started to cool, the time for the next meal arrived. A predictable meal was the order of the day, more pasta and a few beers, then we headed back to the motel, only to decide it was too early to go to bed if we were to ever cure this jet lag, so went in search of another local bar. A few more beers later and we retired to bed. Again we were out like lights, but also, predictably, bug-eyed awake at 3.30am.

With our insomnia we endured the wee small hours in a half sleep and eventually the rest of the world stirred. It was now the eve of the Ironman and there was a lot more to get done so we ate a hearty breakfast and headed up to town. The initial shock of the long climb was slowly receding with each additional drive we took up to Lake Placid. We parked on the outskirts of town and headed for the Ironman Village.

First things first, I had to register for tomorrow's start. Now registration was very cool. In the appropriate tent I found my number, went to the first desk and showed my licence (proud of my International Endorsement). From here I was given a bag and my numbers. Then it was on to the next desk to sign a disclaimer. Then to the next desk to get weighed. Hang on, this is all a bit serious. Finally I had to pick up my Champion Chip. All around me in a quiet intensity other competitors went through the same process. The anticipation was electrifying. Working through the process was strange, almost like a 'go to this desk, then that desk, and then we'll whisk you into space'. It was oddly exhilarating. We could feel the excitement everywhere. All the volunteers were wishing me luck.

Having signed the appropriate forms, stood on scales, had a wrist band clipped on and been wished luck numerous times, I stepped back out into the bright light. Unbelievably, I was registered for the event.

Next up was the bike racking. I wheeled my faithful, shiny new Trek in for the bike inspection. The marshal had a quick look over her and fixed a sticker to the crossbars reading 'Ironman Lake Placid 2001 – Bike Inspection'. You know, however much I have tried, that sticker won't budge, no, not even three years later on. Very, very cool.

I racked my bike in my allocated spot, number 236, deflated the tyres (as they can burst if you leave them in the hot sun at full pressure) and memorised my spot. Tomorrow morning, before all the shenanigans began, I would be back to re-inflate the tyres and put my drink bottles on the frame.

With the morning excitement out of the way, it was time to get down to the serious business of getting my hair cut. I found a traditional barber who had been cutting hair for 70 years using only clippers and a cut-throat razor. 'Oh no, these new contraption scissors things will never catch on' he stated. The results demonstrated that he was a one trick pony. I was delighted with the cut, very little weight to carry on the big day. Linds on the other hand had to double take as I walked back towards her. She described it as a cross between no hair on my head and a fine stubble. I continued to grin from ear to ear, confident that my crew cut would strike fear into the hearts of all but the hardest opponents.

As the sun beat down and the temperature rose, we wandered back into town to find some lunch. Grabbing some bagels, we ate them on a grassy knoll. One never knows what one will see from this kind of vantage point here in the good old US of A. In terms of major news events though, there was nothing much to report, although I kept a sharp eye out for half-open windows in the surrounding buildings. Lunch passed without incident.

Like bar humbugs, we decided to watch rather than participate in the 'Parade of Nations', something which resembled a mini Olympics parade. I know, only in America. There were cheerleaders, a band, state troopers and some soldiers all marching along, followed by the competitors, divided into countries, brandishing their respective flags. Rousing, but at the same time very cheesy. For the few seconds when the UK contingent went by, we wished we had participated but that soon passed. One big bonus of at least lending our clapping support was that I picked up a free, white, Timex sun cap, one of the goodies being thrown out into the crowds. This turned out to be an essential bit of kit, especially with my new go faster barnet. Not that it has to be Timex, but a baseball cap is a must in the heat.

Finally, it was time for the race briefing. We were almost there. The last two days had been the slowest two days of my life. Poor old Linds. I realise at times like these how much she loves me. I could go into the detail of what was covered in the race briefing but I won't. If you're going to do an Ironman, you'll go to one and find out. All I really remembered was 'Don't draft' and then endless questions about what constituted five bike lengths. Err, that'll be the length of five bikes put wheel to wheel in a line. Only in America. The other salient point from the briefing was just how hot the sun was. The 'how hot the sun was' wasn't actually part of the briefing, but more an observation of how hot it was going to be merely from sitting in an uncovered stand. I was going to burn alive thanks to my new buddy, the over-zealous barber.

It was mid-afternoon. We decided to chill out up by Mirror Lake and read our books. Bizarrely, as we sat there, two girls walked by with a ferret on a lead with a little bell attached to its collar. Linds and I just looked at each other. This really was American Pie meets Deliverance. Again, we could almost hear the banjos. We ate early and headed back to the motel to get my transition bags ready.

I know, time must be standing still for you too by now, but it's worth sitting up for a second and taking notes here. You will get a number of bags which can at first be very confusing. Here's what they're for.

Bag 1 - Swim to Bike – fairly self-explanatory. You need your bike bits in here, i.e. helmet, sunglasses, etc. Don't forget some Vaseline and a bottle of energy drink just to swig to replenish yourself after the swim. I also put a bottle of water in, just in case my feet were sandy, so I could get them clean and the sand wouldn't rub. I can be a bit of a princess sometimes, but I wasn't taking any risks.

Bag 2 - Bike Special Needs – you pick this up halfway round the bike course if you need to, although I was to learn that the feedstations provided enough. I put some drink, Tracker bars and gels in here.

Bag 3 – Bike to Run – luxury here, clean socks and more Vaseline. I also put another bottle of energy drink, my new sun cap and some clean sunglasses into this bag. I embarrass myself, I was so precious.

Bag 4 – Run Special Needs – again, anything you think you can absorb on the run if you need additional drinks or food.

Bag 5 – Dry Bag – clothes for after the race. I put some more energy drinks in here, not realising that at that stage, despite the necessity, a sweet carbohydrate drink would be the very last thing on my mind. Actually that's a lie. There would be one thing further from my mind and that would be starting out and doing the whole thing again.

By about 8pm I was all packed and ready to go. My numbers were pinned to my racesuit; goggles, hat and wetsuit were in a neat pile. I was like a live wire. Anticipating this, we had bought a few beers in town. Linds was delighted to have been asked for ID. Not only was she mistaken for a triathlete, she also looked too young to be buying alcohol. Even the beers didn't help me fall asleep. I finally dropped off at midnight. The alarm was set for 4am.

Chapter 32

4am. The Big Day

Ever woken up at 4am? Still felt sleepy when you did? Felt like you've been cheated? Could roll over and close your eyes and fall into a deep, untroubled, blissful sleep? Not me, not on this day. As the alarm sounded I sat bolt upright, not a thought of sleeping on. For me it was show time, time for business. I had slept four hours and felt absolutely wide awake.

It was the bewitching hour. There was a stillness and silence all around me. The room was dark and Linds blissfully slept on. Her normal devotion had waned slightly and she'd asked to be woken just before we headed off to town. With determination she slumbered on through my alarm. But I was awake, I could feel every tingle. The start of Ironman Lake Placid 2001 was three hours away.

First things first. It was time to shatter the stillness and tranquillity. The CD walkman went on. A heavy metal man I have always been and today I needed a good tune in my head. As I did my preparatory bits I kicked off with Slipknot (Reading Festival), Ozzy (Milton Keynes) and Marilyn Manson (the sound track to all my best air guitar and hair brush mic screaming moments). There I was, high in the hills of upstate New York, in a wooden clad motel, sitting on the end of the bed, with Linds fast asleep beside me, heavy metal blasting in my ears, eating a banana, a Tracker, glugging energy drink (I was already starting to go off the taste) and drinking tea, more tea and yet more tea. I needed to get things going downstairs so to speak. Let's just say with two pints of tea in me, everything was working fine. With the first sitting out of the way,

I had a shower and a shave. As I emerged smelling of roses, humming a guitar riff, there was Linds, a little groggy, with another steaming cup of tea for me. Maybe she was more devoted than I gave her credit for. She didn't seem as excited as I was, but then she hadn't enjoyed her first sip of energy drink yet.

I took several trips to the loo as I got ready. Yep, total paranoia. Then it was time to apply lubrication. To avoid blisters and rubs I smeared Vaseline on all moving parts, armpits, back of the knees, chest, between the toes, even a generous helping where the sun don't shine. I pulled on my tri-suit, T-shirt, sweatshirt, rain jacket, socks and sandals. Linds ensured there were lots of photos of me in socks and sandals, obviously more devoted but also more awake than I had thought. Just to stress, socks and sandals is not a combination I put together readily, but I'd only packed one pair of trainers and they were in my 'Bike to Run' bag. I was leaving nothing to chance, even at the risk of making some massive fashion faux pas.

At 5.15am we headed off to Lake Placid. It was still dark, but as we climbed higher the mountains became silhouetted by a half-lit, reddish sky. In Linds' words, it was 'horrendously early' but there were a lot of people on the move. We pulled into Lake Placid at 5.45, just as the sun started to glimmer over the rooftops. It was going to be a big day.

I calculated there were 75 minutes to the start. How was I feeling? I think surfers call it stoked. I was stoked, I had butterflies in my stomach and my senses were jangling. How best to describe my emotions? I went off to find the loo again.

By 6am the temperature was pleasantly warm. Around town there was a supercharged buzz, folks walking around wild eyed with anticipation. In front of the Ironman Village the marshals were numbering competitors with big black markers. I stripped down and '236' was printed on both arms and legs. I was bursting, I felt good, ready to go. All of a sudden time was moving extra fast. I went into the Ironman Village and dropped my transition bags at the appropriate places. Then it was over to my bike to pump up the tyres and load my two energy bottles on board.

I felt like pinching myself as I stood there in the middle of the bike racking area. Here I was, under clear blue skies, in the middle of the Ironman Village, in upstate New York, with less than 45 minutes to the start of an actual Ironman race. I couldn't have been further away from my garden seat, sweating away reading about others' adventures. Here I was in the middle of my own. I knew today would be a significant day in my life. One I would always remember, a kind of watershed, a changing of perspective. On that very profound thought, I went off to find the loo again.

At 6.25 we went up to Mirror Lake. It was down to business. I dropped off both my Bike and Run Special Need Bags, left Linds with my remaining gear and went for a quick warm up run. I stopped by a deserted old building and had a really long pee. I was confident I wasn't starting the race dehydrated. I jogged back to Linds, then back again to the building to have another long pee. Where was it coming from?

Mirror Lake was packed out with people by this time. I had a quick stretch by Linds and the minutes sped along. The butterflies by this stage had transformed into bats, beating away inside. At 6.35 I pulled on my wetsuit, carefully soaking the backs of my knees, elbows, shoulders and neck with baby oil. I kissed Linds and headed for the water with my goggles and hat.

I coached myself, get in the water, swim about, calm the nerves. The memories of Bournemouth were still vivid; the cold, the breathlessness, the panic. At 6.45 I waded into Mirror Lake. To my relief the water was unnaturally warm. I didn't want to contemplate why in the shallows, but needless to say I kept my mouth firmly closed and swam out. There was going to be no repeat of Bournemouth today. My plan was stay out of trouble during the swim. This would be a mass start with over 1,800 competitors. Back in July 2001 it was the largest mass start ever in triathlon (a total that is regularly beaten these days). I reasoned it was going to be a long day so best to stay out of the thick of it. I only realised later as the gun sounded that most of the field had had the same thought, so, through our own caution, we all ended up right in the thick of it.

I saw Linds one final time and gave her a wave. She seemed to be engrossed in conversion, obviously imparting pearls of wisdom of the whys and wherefores of these things, quite the expert compared to some of these novice spectators.

As we waited for the count we paddled back and forth, treading water. The sky was a brilliant blue, the lake ahead was perfectly still, a low mist hung just above the water, the banks were lined with spectators four to five people deep. As a lone music teacher sang the national anthem, the air was electric. Over 1,800 neoprene clad athletes, treading water and waiting.

And then the gun went off......

Chapter 33

Mirror Lake

There was a surge and then there was mayhem. The calm of Mirror Lake erupted. Bodies drove forwards, a sea of arms, legs, torsos, white water, black neoprene. I kicked with my legs and pulled with my arms, as I breathed the white water that filled the air. I had never been in anything like it. Everyone squeezed together. Hold your water, swim, stroke, kick, breathe.

With most races the initial mayhem calms after maybe 30 seconds. Not today. Every few strokes a body passed in front of me, an arm pushed down my legs, another across my back. I was kicked hard in the face, there was a whack on my hand. Just keep swimming.

The pack moved forward in this jostling, crushed fashion. I tried to get a rhythm, pull with the arms, kick with the legs, breathe. The squeeze didn't ease. It was just a mass of bodies. As I breathed to the right a helicopter hovered above filming, its blades whooshing the air. As we moved forward, it slid sideways with the field. If I hadn't realised before, I knew now that this race was the big time. As we crept on so did the helicopter. Despite the chaos, in fact because of the chaos, I was loving it.

The field stayed tight up to the top of the rectangular course. There was a shoving and pushing as we turned through 90 degrees around each buoy and then it settled down as we headed back to town and the halfway point. The field stretched out slowly. I was being carried along by my own elation. Here I was racing, in crystal clear warm waters, with a helicopter hovering above me. I coached myself on, 'Okay 17 minutes and you'll have done another quarter, you can swim 17 minutes continuously no problem, hey that's only just over 30 lengths'.

I settled down and kept up with those around me. Stroke, stroke, breathe. The course slid behind me and suddenly reeds reared up from the lake floor below my outstretched hand. My feet went down, hit sand and I waded forward onto the beach. The cheers of the crowd on the beach were phenomenal. I ran forward through the champion chip checkpoint, across the 20 feet of sand and back into the water for lap two. As I waded out I checked my split, 35 minutes. That lifted me. I dived forward and started to swim again.

'Two sets of 17 minutes and the swim is over,' my inner voice egged me on.

I settled down again. As I passed the end of the town jetty I could see the bubbles of the safety divers below. Reassuring.

Up the length of Mirror Lake I swam again. This would be a lonelier lap as the field had thinned. Needless to say, I still had company. Slowly we moved forward. All along the bank spectators cheered. 'Linds is somewhere there', I thought. Again I smiled. I couldn't believe it, here I was, right in the thick of my dream. I tried to stay to the side of the group on the second lap to avoid any more kicks or thumps. I regretted this as I weaved my way up and down the course with less people to take a bearing from. I tried to get back into the group but my second lap ended up being less purposeful than my first.

Up along the third quarter, to the first buoy, along the short top section to the last buoy and back down the final stretch. The last 700 metres dragged a little and I started to shift my mind to the transition and the bike. Finally the bed of the lake reared up below me again, a few more strokes and my hands felt weeds. As my feet touched the sandy beach I stood and the swim was over. I felt it had gone in the blink of an eye, but it had actually taken 1 hour and 12 minutes. The bit I had dreaded for 12 months was behind me. Wow. I stumbled forward, over the champion chip split pad and the noise filled my ears again. Cheering, clapping, encouragement, the crowd were ecstatic. As I crossed the pad, I thought of Mum and Dad, who would see my split time thousands of miles away at their home in Chile as they followed the live coverage on the 'Ironmanlive.com' web site. I also found out later my boss, Gordon, had logged on and was following my progress.

But hell, no time to dwell. I ran forward to the wetsuit stripping area where strong handed volunteers helped me wrestle my suit off. I couldn't believe the cheering and the noise. I thanked my helper and ran down along the matting towards transition, lined six deep either side with wild spectators. It was electrifying. About halfway down I saw Linds, gave her a big smile and we high fived. I think she guessed I was all right. With all her yelling and bobbing up and down she certainly had far more energy than at 4.30am. I hardly realised at the time but she was going through her own transition to 'Hardcore Ironman Supporter', holding her own endurance vigil. There was none of this wandering off to potter around town for her. Only later would I come to understand the full extent of her, 'Way to go', 'Keep going', 'Good job'. She was as wild-eyed as the rest. The atmosphere down those 300 metres to the transition area was incredible.

I ran into the Ironman Village and into the 'Swim to Bike' bag storage area. I quickly found number '236' and headed for the change tent. The tent was packed, but I found some floor space and emptied my bag. In it I shoved my wetsuit, goggles and hat. A little flustered, I coached myself, 'slow down', Ian's words came back, the 'longer the race, the slower the transition'. I mentally settled myself down. I took a swig from my energy bottle and carefully made sure that I did everything right. A helper smothered my back in suncream. Methodically, I checked my feet were clean and rinsed off any dirt with the bottle of water I had packed for this purpose. I pulled on my socks and cycling shoes. I took another swig from my energy bottle and loaded some energy bars in my back pocket. Then it was on with my cycling gloves, helmet and sunglasses and suddenly I had no reason to be in the change tent anymore. Swept along by the crowd of athletes, I jogged through into the bike racking area in the middle of the Ironman Village. With great efficiency, as I left the tent a volunteer read my number into a walkie talkie. This was relayed to another volunteer near to where my bike was. She pulled it from the stand and as I reached my row there was my shiny Trek waiting for me. At full canter I pushed it through on to the mounting area, climbed aboard and was off.

The swim had been awesome. The first lap had been like a street fight carried out in the front crawl position. With the overhead helicopter, the surge, the foaming water and the crowds it had been more than I had hoped for and much less than I had dreaded. I just focused on swimming, holding my place and moving forward. Linds said that from the bank it was an amazing sight. The transition from calm to absolute charged white water was instant. She also said it was heart breaking. Within the first few metres a female competitor pulled up. The field surged on and she swam to a jetty. She climbed up and just sat there crying.

I was oblivious to this as I headed away from Lake Placid, with 112 miles of road stretching before me.

Chapter 34

Revelation On The Hot Road To Black Brook

The start of the bike course was quick. The road fell away from the transition area, down the side of the school and, after a few tight turns, I was quickly passing through the outskirts of downtown Lake Placid and then onto the main highway.

The countryside started to open up. The noise and the cheering were gone and, with only the Trek humming below me, some six hours of cycling lay before me. Sobering.

A clear blue sky stretched from horizon to horizon, the Olympic ski jumps flew by, roads lined with pine forests rolled below my wheels. I swept past the police roadblocks, along the undulating highway.

I coached myself, 'Keep feeding'. I reached down to my bottle cage and took a long draught of energy drink. As the temperature started to rise, I was already going off its sweetness. This didn't bode well. I took another swig.

The road was super smooth, perfect for cycling. I shifted lower onto my aerobars and started to settle into a rhythm. From the very start the drafting rule seemed a little ludicrous. Unsurprising, the field, this far behind the pros, was three deep with riders. Keeping the mandatory distance ahead and behind was impossible. I had wanted to race a 'pure' race and not to draft. Initially I tried overtaking people or dropping back, but my efforts were to no avail. In the end I settled for where I was and to satisfy my troubled conscience tried to ensure I was in the wind as much as possible. These early miles fell away. I had a good pace and despite the rolling route, overall we were enjoying more downhill than uphill. I tried not to worry about how this height would be regained. Live for the moment, I reasoned, with gallows humour.

There were constant reminders that this race was about more than endurance. I passed and was passed by freshly bloodied legs and arms and half torn shorts from scrapes and falls. 'Be alert' I warned myself, Mum's sensible voice in my ear. On one part, as the field whooshed down a long, smooth descent all fairly close together and travelling at a speed in the mid 40 miles per hour, we all sat up as we passed an ambulance, lights ablaze, tending to two bloodied riders whose bikes were left mangled around the crash barriers. I could hear Mum's warnings and vigilantly watched the road, rear wheels and riders ahead of me.

As I pedalled, I continued to drink. The energy drink was becoming less and less palatable. I told myself to feed. I was amazed as we came to our first town outside Lake Placid. It was Saturday morning, about 9am now and already the crowds were out. People sat in their gardens, cheering, ringing bells, waving placards wishing us well. One banner stuck in my mind,

'See you in 56 miles.'

I took another swig of the now sickly sweet fluid in my bottle cage. The Trek and I pushed on. Every 6 miles there was another feedstation and to keep everything tidy you dropped your wrappers and bottles within eyesight of the feedstation. To me, trying to hit the bins with my empties at least added a dimension of fun. At the first station I duly complied, noting to my dismay that, despite my best efforts, I had only managed half a bottle of energy drink and had not even touched the second I was carrying. Was I taking on enough fuel? I grabbed a fresh bottle, stored it quickly and then grabbed two sachets of energy gel. I bit into the top of the gel and squeezed it into my mouth. I figured the key with feedstations was slowing down and making sure I got what I wanted. Many a time I saw a speedy rider grab from the volunteers, drop their treasure and curse the poor volunteer. As I rode away I bit into the second gel and squeezed it into my mouth, washing them both down with energy drink. Mmmm, finally I had discovered the true breakfast of champions.

The route was breathtaking, mostly lined with pines and other evergreen trees. We passed perfectly still lakes reflecting the sky and surrounding hills, meandering lazy streams and fast-flowing torrents. Big hills and mountains lined the horizon either side and jagged cliffs reared up without warning, leaning over the road. The road surface was flat and smooth and the Trek hummed effortlessly forward.

It was still early in the day, well, it's all relative, having had a 4am start, and I was enjoying the ride. I felt good, the bike was shifting, my average speed was 20 to 21 miles per hour. Was I overcooking it? I wasn't sure. The buzz of being in an Ironman had passed. I no longer had to pinch myself to check it wasn't a dream. I was well aware I was in one as I worked to get the miles behind me.

Again, at the next feedstation, despite my best efforts to polish off the devil's favourite drink, I had only managed another half bottle. I figured if I wasn't going to drink all the energy there was little point in carrying two bottles, so I dispensed with the half full one, keeping the one from the previous feedstation, and took on some water. I reasoned if I drank energy drink with water I would ensure I was hydrated. It would be easier on the stomach and taste less intense. I also grabbed two gels and half a banana, thanking the volunteers who were eagerly handing them out. As I accelerated away, I mashed the banana in my mouth and stowed the gels away in my pocket.

Since the long descent where the crash had been, the route had been fairly flat, winding along a valley. However, shortly after the feedstation the course took a sharp left and headed to Wilmington and our motel. As the route reared upwards, riders were standing on their pedals, me included, pulling our bikes up the slope. Steadily we climbed up to the ridge. It was a long climb. Once we had crested the ridge, we sped down into Wilmington. For me it was here that the Ironman truly began as we headed out of town on a long dogleg, 5 miles out and 5 miles back on the hot road to Black Brook.

The day was heating up. As cyclists passed me on their return leg, 10 miles ahead of me, the realisation truly started to dawn that this was going to be a very long day. Don't get me wrong, I was still loving it, but the euphoria of being in an Ironman had died and now the realisation that I would have to graft to complete this was very clear. With every turn of the pedal the inescapable thought grew within me, I was cycling away from Lake Placid, I still had a 7 mile climb even before the halfway point, and then I would have to ride it all again on the second lap. The mind games had begun. I should have realised, in a funny way, I was actually moving closer to Lake Placid. As I pedalled on I knew I was going to have to look deep inside. I would work, suffer and hurt a lot before the end. With this came its own satisfaction.

A few miles on I stopped for a pee. I pulled up my short leg and peed for England. It was clear and there was plenty of it. I knew I was drinking enough. The stop also put some life back into my legs. But, true to say, I no longer experienced the Trek surging forward on the road. The gradient rolled up and down and the temperature had climbed rapidly in the foot of the valley. I pedalled on, continually reaching down to glug more energy drink, horrible stuff though it was by now.

However, it wasn't all doom and gloom on the hot road to Black Brook. One supporter's sign stuck out on its own as the road passed under dense trees. It read, 'And this one time at band camp…' For those who've seen 'American Pie' you'll understand this. With no one around, I laughed out loud.

Eventually, I rounded the hairpin turn at Black Brook and started heading back towards Wilmington. The continuous line of people going the other way lifted me. As I passed back though Wilmington I ensured I fuelled up before the long climb to Lake Placid. I sped past our motel and gave the owners a wave. They had a placard for all their guests who were racing and gave me a big cheer. It sounds odd, but all the support really lifted the spirits.

And then the 7 miles of climbing began. It was a long climb up a spectacular mountain river and gully. I knocked back some more energy drink. The gradient was steady, but to my relief what I had missed in the car were the flats and the odd downhill bits. Halfway up was another feedstation and then the road stretched on and up. This was Ironman, gullies, waterfalls, fast flowing rapids, sheer rock faces, ski lifts stretching away from the road, climbing.

Eventually the familiar outskirts of town appeared and I was cycling past the sprinklers of Lake Placid Golf Course. Almost halfway. As we climbed the final bit into town towards Mirror Lake the atmosphere was supercharged. The road was four deep with crowds either side for the final 400 metres of the climb, narrowing the route as we rode through. The supporters were going wild, cheering, clapping, ringing bells. It was like a mountain finish on the Tour de France. As I rode through, the somewhat short hairs on the back of my neck raised with the energy and emotion. This was Ironman.

The route swept past Mirror Lake, down by the 'Bike Special Needs' bag pick up. I loaded some bits and pedalled on. There was Linds, at the top of Mirror Lake, where the swim start had been, standing on a big rock. I waved and smiled. She was leaping up and down, wild-eyed. I wasn't sure who would be worse off at the end of the day, me the competitor or Linds the ardent spectator.

The bike route passed through the town centre and with a beep of my champion chip I started my second lap. On we rode, down past the Ice Rink, past transition and the Ironman Village, down by the school and then back out through downtown Lake Placid, past the Olympic Ski Jump Centre.

56 miles to go. The last 2 miles up through the crowds into town had been awesome, the energy and support inspiring and maybe, just maybe I had overcooked it. I had maybe got a little carried away and as I rode out of town my energy just seemed to seep away. Suddenly I felt empty.

I looked at my watch. 2 hours and 45 minutes for lap one. That was quick. Too quick?

I reached down and drank some more energy drink. As the juice hit my stomach, I felt a cramp. I felt sick and nauseous. Oh no. I pedalled on a little panicked. I knew how hard the last lap had been, another 56 miles and then the small matter of a marathon to run. I had to fuel but the energy drink wasn't working.

At the next feedstation I grabbed as many gels as I could, a banana and a bottle of water. I drank as much water as I could, hoping it would ease the stomach. Miraculously it seemed to do the trick. I bit open a gel, squeezed it out and washed it down with more water. The cramps disappeared. I pushed on, continuing in this vein; water, gels, banana and the odd sip of energy drink, my speed slower and my strength noticeably less. Trees shaded the route and as it passed away from town, the miles fell behind me. Down the long descent I sped, coaching myself 'Concentrate, you're tired now.' On to the flat, mile after mile, this was Ironman. My fear of drafting violations long gone, I was on my own, or at least that was how it felt.

I realised the second lap was going to be tough and uncomfortable. I had become less aware of the views. It was a blur. I just pedalled, changed gear, chatted to myself and reminded myself to eat. I shifted my riding position periodically to save my arms, back, hamstrings and neck. Every so often I would stop for a pee, still reassuringly clear. I was drinking plenty.

As the route veered left and rose up the long climb to the ridge above

Wilmington, the balls of my feet just at the point of the pedal crank really started to ache. Every turn of the pedal was like having a hot nail pushed into the sole of my foot. As I stood to take on the climb every turn was agony. My options? Keep on pedalling. This was Ironman.

Into Wilmington and the long dogleg to Black Brook. It was hotter and stiller now. Just keep going, keep fuelling. I passed the 'Band Camp' sign again. I smiled but didn't laugh this time. The soles of my feet were agony. Around the hairpin and back to Wilmington, My face, hands, arms and legs were sticky with gels, roasted by the sun, my neck and back were aching, I was tired and my bum hurt. Each downwards stroke of the pedal hurt. My glasses were streaked with sweat and my racesuit was dry and salty.

The romance was gone, but it was replaced by something better. I pushed myself on, 'This isn't supposed to be easy.'

As I neared Wilmington for the last time my spirits lifted. When I hit the bottom of the final climb I knew I had 40 minutes left on my bike. I started climbing with four riders and we all obviously felt the same. The tempo picked up as we took each other's pace. We climbed in and out of the saddle. We had purpose and were heading for Lake Placid town.

Halfway up, on a steep incline, we passed a girl in a bikini sunning herself on a rock. She cheered us on, 'Way to go', and lifted her bikini top as we rode by. We smiled, a few words were passed in the group and we silently got back to work.

The climb slowly dropped behind us. Up past the golf course, the short electrifying rise to the top of Mirror Lake and then we were coasting down its far side. It was a relief to be back in town. As we rolled down beside the invitingly cool lake there was Linds standing on her rock enthusiastically cheering riders on. I was glad to see she was keeping her top on. The swim had taken me 1 hour and 12 minutes; the whole ride was just under 6 hours. In total she had been cheering for 7 hours and 15 minutes. Her support was extreme.

I had slowed considerably on the second lap, especially on the second half of it, mainly due to the pain in my feet. I put it down to the heat, my feet swelling and my shoes being too tight. I've since replaced the shoes for a slightly bigger, airier pair and also loosened the tightness on my pedals, allowing my feet to float a little more. Loosening the pedals really did the trick. To this day I still get pains occasionally, but a quick quarter to half turn with an Allen key on the pedals to loosen them slightly solves it.

In the end the bike course finished very quickly. We came into town, past the Olympic Ice Rink and the school and suddenly I was dismounting. Wow, I had survived the swim and the bike.

I passed my beloved Trek to a volunteer, glad (I never thought I would say it) to see it carried away. I sprinted to pick up my 'Bike to Run' transition bag.

Chapter 35

Chicken Soup In The Rain

Not really. Do you honestly think I sprinted? No, that was what my head told my legs to do, but my legs and back had other plans. It was more of a limp and a hobble, a quickish, tottering stumble that took me towards my transition bag. Hang on a second, this limping gait wasn't in my plan.

I took my bag into the transition tent and found a seat. Ahhh, absolute bliss. My legs hurt, I was a little giddy from the heat and my feet and back ached. What a pleasure to stop. The tent was cool and quiet and still. Heaven.

Another 26.2 miles stretched out ahead of me. Here in the cool, sitting with my aching self, they seemed long miles indeed. It was amazing I didn't stop. In truth, it didn't even cross my mind. I had been behaving abnormally for so long, to keep going was the only natural course of action. Instinctively I reached into my bag, pulled out my trainers, clean socks, Vaseline and sun cap. I unclipped my helmet, unstrapped the torture devices which until now I had mistaken for cycling shoes and peeled off my socks. A volunteer asked whether I needed a hand.

'No, no, just taking it easy, no rush.' Ian's transition advice echoing in my mind again. The volunteer offered me a shoulder massage. Now we're talking, to hell with any English reserve.

'Yes please.'

It was great to be out of the sun and, with a rub of the shoulders, my back pain eased off. I reached forward, smeared my toes with Vaseline, one sock, two, one trainer, two, sun cap on, helmet and cycling shoes in the bag. I opted to keep my smeared Oakleys on despite the sweat streaks and then, all of a sudden, I had no reason to be sitting in the cool, quiet, changing tent.

I stood, thanked the volunteer and headed for the door, ready to face the heat. At the exit from the Ironman Village there was a feedstation. I drank some water and energy drink. From the very start I had wondered what embarking on the marathon would feel like. There is a picture of me leaving transition that says it all. My face shows a grimace as I try to get my stiff legs going, each step fighting gravity. Setting out was hard, daunting and massive. One foot in front of the next, my strategy was to just point myself towards the next feedstation a mile down the road.

As the Ironman Village slowly disappeared behind me, the stiffness from the ride eased. I was no longer limping and hobbling, but to describe it as much above a jog would be generous. In fact it was more of a shuffle. I had been awake for a good while now. I had woken at 4am, started racing at 7am and it was now 2.30 in the afternoon. The road stretched out before me, step by step passing below me. Stick to the plan. Now, the original plan had been to run, but I settled for either a jog or a shuffle between feedstations. At each feedstation, I would walk through picking up a cup of energy (somehow referring to energy drink as energy made it more palatable) and a cup of water. I'd drink both as I walked to the end of the feedstation and then run, jog, shuffle to the next station a mile further down the road. I figured 26 feedstations later I would be victorious. Well, that was the plan.

The marathon route quickly cut out of town, down a sharp descent. I had the sense to realise this descent would loom ahead of me at about mile 12 and mile 25. Best not look too far ahead. The route passed out through downtown Lake Placid, past the Olympic Ski Jump station and over the bridge where state troopers had stopped the traffic, lights flashing, many hours earlier. All this scenery had seemed to whiz past on the bike, but everything was relative, I guess. Here the route forked to the left, running past pine forests and green fields to the eventual turn point, marking the halfway point of the lap.

I just remember jogging on and on and on. It took an eternity to reach this turn point. I couldn't even think as far as the second lap. Despite time standing still on lap one, all in all my plan was going well. I was in good spirits. Every mile I would walk, drink and chat merrily to the volunteers on each feedstation. There was an amazing camaraderie in the field. At this point, as we moved forward together, each of us at our own ultra-shuffle terminal velocities, finishing was all that mattered. Places were irrelevant, therefore everyone tried to lift everyone else. As we moved along there was chat, banter and a great warm spirit. Looking back, my brain was so addled I can barely remember a single conversation, but I do remember smiling, chatting to some and moving on and cheering others as they eased past. I couldn't really describe anyone but I had an overriding feeling of not being alone. Here again was the spirit of Ironman.

The first turn point was tough mentally. Three quarters of a marathon still to go and that first quarter sure as hell was hard. Less than 7 miles covered. I put that behind me and shuffled on, the tall Olympic Ski Jump hill slowly drawing closer and closer, and then the outskirts of town, the steep incline up to the Ironman Village and up to Mirror Lake and Linds standing vigilantly on her rock.

The first half of the marathon took me 2 hours. I was very pleased. I had been on the go for some 9 and a half hours. As I crested the rise to the banks of Mirror Lake, there was Linds cheering from her rock, unflagging. I realised it must be love. I slowed, checked she was okay, we kissed and I shuffled on. 13 miles to go.

As I ran back down Mirror Lake, I saw a heartbreaking accident. A disobedient kid had run out in front of a cyclist, who was obviously doing his best to beat the 10 hour cut off. He flew over his handlebars and crashed onto the road. I was feeling exhausted and I was halfway through the marathon. At this point in the day, finishing was everything. Having dedicated 12 months of my life to Ironman, my heart really went out to this guy. I hoped he got up.

As I passed the Ironman Village the route split. One sign read, 'To the finish', and the other read, 'Second Lap'. 13.1 miles still lay before me. I plodded on, head down towards the next feedstation. It was here that the wheels on my chariot started to wobble. As the Olympic Ski Jump passed by on my right, step-by-step the energy drained away and I started to slow. I willed myself on, but despite my resolve there was little left, the engine felt like it was running on fumes. Comfortingly, there were others around experiencing the same. One guy advised walking the hills and drinking the chicken soup and coke on the feedstations. With nothing to lose I took a cup of chicken soup at the next station. Heaven. Nothing could describe it. It wasn't sweet, it wasn't sickly, just delicious and warm. My spirits rose. I left the station with renewed vigour. Another mile and there would be some more soup.

On the second lap, the marathon just became a battle of attrition, survival. I shuffled, I walked. Initially just on the hills, but then on parts of the flats. It was tough. The run became a blur. As the evening drew in the feedstations passed by. Chicken soup was consumed with relish. I was peeing well. As the light faded I ran over the champion chip mat on the turn point of the second lap and someone called, 'We're going home'. I smiled, those words meant a lot. I fixed my sights on the Ski Jump and slowly reeled it in. As I alternated between shuffling and walking I developed a cheeseburger fantasy. That was all I wanted. It started to rain, lightly, then heavily but I hardly noticed. I just moved forward towards my next cup of chicken soup.

The Ski Jump eventually came up alongside and passed by my left shoulder. My spirits lifted. I had arrived back on the outskirts of town on the last lap of an actual Ironman. The day had been even harder than I imagined but, as I passed the first houses it dawned on me, I was going to be an Ironman. I felt elated, but nothing got easier. I shuffled on. Over the last few miles I remember experiencing a roller coaster of emotions. My body wanted to finish, but emotionally I wanted to hold the moment, for it not to finish, to keep living the feeling I was enjoying. Despite all the toil, I had loved every second. The rain was heavy now. I crested the rise to Mirror Lake and there was Linds on her rock, a little bedraggled from the rain. Beyond her was the final turnaround. The second lap had taken me 3 hours. I stopped by her rock, gave her a kiss and a hug and told her I loved her. I really meant it, there were tears behind my glasses.

I shuffled on, up around the final turn point and back down along Mirror Lake. My pace lifted. With less than a mile to go I actually started to run. I was going to finish. Unbelievable. As I neared the filter lane a runner next to me said, 'Need to do a half-marathon in 4 and half hours, I should be alright.'

'Of course you will, no problem.'

He peeled off to the left, he'd make it I was sure, and I went to the right down the finishers lane and into the stadium.

I was lifted, I was flying along, the hurt was gone, the fatigue evaporated. I kid you not, I was sprinting, well, running fast. I came around the track, between the grandstands. The rain poured down, my arms pumped. There was the finish.

I raised my arms and crossed the line.

Chapter 36

Finisher

Wow. What a feeling. I stood on the finisher podium, arms raised, the photographer's camera flashed. Ironman. For me, on that podium, with the Ironman course immediately behind me, that was a moment, an indescribable moment in time, that I will carry with me always. One of the proudest of my life. I had finished in 12 hours 34 minutes 39 seconds. In truth the time was irrelevant. I had completed an Ironman. I was over the moon. A volunteer took my arm, gave me my 'Finisher' T-shirt and medal and another wrapped a towel around my shoulders.

'How do you feel?'

'Great,' I replied.

'Are you sure?'

'No problems at all,' I replied. The comprehension of my achievement beaming across my face. I had finished. I was an Ironman.

'Do you want to go to the medical tent?'

'No really I'm fine, just hungry.'

'Food this way.'

And with that she walked me to the pizza tent. I hadn't realised how hungry I was until, hardly pausing for breath, I wolfed down three large slices of pizza. Each slice literally went in a few mouthfuls. I quickly gulped down a drink, I can't remember what. I had to find Linds. She was as elated as I was, a true 'Ironmate'. On her advice I pulled on my dry clothes. The adrenaline was dying away and the fatigue and stiffness were starting to catch up with me. As the skies really opened, we (well

I) limped back to the car, both of us still grinning like Cheshire cats. It was now time to get the priorities straight, time for that cheeseburger.

I sat in the car, it was a joy to be sitting down, my head hit the head rest and I don't remember much more. The intention had been to grab a bite to eat, a beer and then go back to cheer the last finishers. But Linds saw I was spark out. In fact she couldn't get a word out of me outside MacDonald's, I don't even remember her waking me. She reversed the car and headed for our motel. I was spent, sparko, totally out of it. The build up, the pre-race tension, the early starts induced by jet lag and the race had finally caught up with me. I barely remember getting back to the motel. I lay on the bed fully dressed and there I woke 10 hours later, tired, stiff from head to toe but still smiling.

I remembered why. Ironman.

And Then...?

Pushing myself lies at the very centre of my life. It gives me substance and real purpose, it feeds my spirit and makes me who I am. In a funny way, crossing the finish line at Lake Placid changed me. It sounds weird but it was a watershed, a kind of Rubicon in my life. I don't think it was the Ironman that changed me as much as the process I had gone through. Frustrated with my level of challenge, I had got up out of my back garden and done something about it. Finishing Ironman Lake Placid was one of the proudest moments of my life at that point. But what was really reassuring was that I didn't stay satisfied for long. Another road stretched out ahead. The days following the Ironman were quite sobering. Over the following week the elation and satisfaction slowly receded. What was next?

When we got home, I dutifully logged on to 'Ironmanlive.com' and looked up Ironman Lanzarote, 'the world's toughest Ironman', it read. That should do it. I punched in my credit card details, and suddenly everything was Technicolor again.

Since completing Lake Placid the last three years have flown by. I went on to successfully finish Ironman Lanzarote, although the proverbial wheels wobbled a bit a quarter of the way through the marathon. Another long walk stretched out ahead. I finished in 13 hours 32 minutes.

To date I have completed six Ironman distance triathlons. It was at my third in Switzerland where I learned that I could actually run the whole marathon, a major psychological breakthrough that saw me cross the line in 12 hours 26 minutes, a whole 8 minutes faster than Lake Placid. A new personal best.

After Switzerland I made perhaps the best investment I have ever made in triathlon. I took Ian, of gearsandtears.com fame, on as a coach. He essentially sets out a structured weekly training plan tailored specifically for me. I follow the plan and feedback on what I actually do, heart rate data, times, thoughts, sleep patterns, etc. This ensures I train consistently (in terms of structured sessions rather than what takes my fancy), progressively and, most critically, I avoid the roller coaster of over-training. After diligently following Ian's plan for 12 months I posted 11 hours 53 minutes on a very tough course at Ironman France. My marathon split was just over 4 hours! Then a month later I raced The Longest Day (an Ironman distance race) in Wolverhampton and knocked out a finishing time of 11 hours and 1 minute. I was gutted not to go under 11 hours. But as ever, when the pain of those final miles had subsided, you couldn't wipe the grin off my face. My marathon had taken 3 hours and 53 minutes.

If you're going to invest any money in triathlon and you don't know what you're doing, you won't go far wrong investing in a good, qualified, triathlon specific coach. I reason it costs less than half the monthly membership of a gym and the gains are well worth it. Last year I broke the 11 hour mark, finishing in 10 hours 53 minutes at Ironman Austria. Again, the grin was indelible.

Life has also brought other changes as Linds and I have started a family. Ben has successfully turned our lives upside down for the best part of half a year. The change of perspective, closeness and laughs he has brought are beyond description. At eight weeks old he was dragged out to watch his first Ironman in Austria. All in all, he was suitably under-whelmed by the whole affair. Perhaps Ironman isn't a big enough challenge for him. I must try not to be a competitive Dad.

The year leading up to Lake Placid had been a rich, life changing year for me, with some real tests, figuring a way forward when things got tough. Mostly, it made me appreciate what a true friend Linds is. As I have written this I realise the sacrifices she made, how selfish I was and how selfless she is. People ask, how do you live with him? I don't know either, but I know I'm very lucky. She sent me an e-mail the other day that read, 'There's a thin line between hobby and mental illness'.

But who wants to behave 'Normally'?

Printed in the United Kingdom
by Lightning Source UK Ltd.
121609UK00001B/105/A